LISTEN TO ME

Thanks for your
support

Lynne Bodurt

Listen To Me is a nonfiction memoir.

Library of Congress Cataloging-in-Publication Data is available

ISBN 978-1-7376668-2-0

ISBN (eBook) 978-1-7376668-3-7

Printed in the United States of America

Book cover design: Andi Cuba

Interior design: Lauren Dickerson

ACKNOWLEDGMENTS

From the beginning, Bruce's birth had the most profound influence over my life, more than anyone else. Yes, there was pain, fear, anxiety, the feelings of abandonment, and alienation. However, where he was concerned, there was never uncertainty or hopelessness. Brucie added a level of love and joy to everyone whose life he touched. He gave me another family, including my soul sister, Janice, to whom I am bonded for life, and for whom I am eternally grateful.

This book is my thank you, first and foremost, to David, my first little brother, ever faithful and trusting. No matter what was asked of you, we were always in this together. His wife Lisa and her family/posse are an amazing group of people who welcomed Brucie with wide open arms and lots of love. David is lucky to have you.

To my children: Jerica, no matter your schedule, you were always available for Sunday dinners with your uncle because they were important to me, then consults and support chats, knowing I would never fall apart but giving me permission to just in case; Randy, from a young age you knew what your uncle needed and never flinched from the responsibility; and Laurie, even with working full time from home and homeschooling Maddie and Emily, no FaceTime requests or Zoom invitations were treated as an inconvenience. To Arielle and Robyn, our devoted nieces who kept our spirits up with texts about family and silly things, just because that is what is needed every once in a while. My husband Big Bruce (so ordained by Brucie), you opened your heart from the very beginning, willingly, knowing how important Brucie was to me.

To my KenCrest family: Chuck, Latoya, Ms. Lee, Cedric, and so many others, who loved and cared for my brother and me for 48 years of our lives. Families with whom you are involved are so blessed to have you in their lives. To the ladies in my South Florida Transition Network Chapter, especially Joan, Rory, Judy, Cynthia, Mary, Susan, Susan and Ronnie (my faithful Transition Network Peer Group); to my Paloma family; and to my friends who could not be with me in person yet showed their support with generous contributions to Special Olympics, a wonderful organization for those with special needs in which my brother was involved for years. To my editor Proofreader Sandi whose gentle persuasion helped bring this story to fruition. To Lauren Dickerson and Andi Cuba, my amazing dynamic duo of Socialbooks Agency, without whom there would be no book or social media. Last but not least, to the wonderful doctors and nurses at Temple University Hospital. Your commitment of care to Brucie and me was given without hesitation. It has restored my faith in the care of those who may need extra help.

~

PREFACE

"To know Bruce, was to love him."

I hadn't gone looking to write a book. And although I love to write, especially poetry, writing can be arduous and was never cathartic for me. But sometimes something or someone touches your heart, your deepest soul, and you just know their story needs to be told. For those who have lived with, loved, and lost handicapped siblings, I share your pain and revel in your joys.

This is that story.

LISTEN TO ME

HOW MY DOWN SYNDROME BROTHER SAVED MY LIFE

LYNNE PODRAT

CONTENTS

"You never know how
strong you are
until being strong is all you
have."

Bob Marley

INTRODUCTION

My new normal as my brother Bruce's guardian was to wake up every morning at 5:00 a.m. Mountain Time so I could speak with the nurses by 7:00 a.m. Eastern Standard Time for updates on the previous night and a course of action for that day, including dialysis, permission for test approval, permission for procedural approval, numbers, or notes from the doctor. My husband and I were in Vail, Colorado, where we spend our summers, and my brother Brucie, who had Down syndrome was staying at the Ken-Crest group home in Philadelphia at the time.

It was July 2020 when Janice, his primary caretaker, called to tell me Bruce was being taken to the hospital. The dialysis center was very concerned with his numbers and insisted he go immediately. Dialysis takes a toll on blood count and blood pressure, so I was not immediately alarmed. This had happened before. I was FaceTiming with Bruce when he learned he would be admitted for what was explained as gallbladder issues. His bile numbers were high, and his skin was yellow.

My father died of pancreatic cancer, so I was wary of the symptoms. I called my daughter, Jerica, a second-year surgical resident at Houston Methodist to discuss my own theory. Bruce spent three days in the hospital alone due to COVID where I was never able to speak with him. The nurses were too busy to speak with me, but I was able to speak with his doctors. When they learned no one was able to communicate with my brother, they filed a complaint with the hospital.

I may have been isolated in Vail, unable to visit due to COVID, but never alone. Latoya, KenCrest's nurse assigned to the Linden Avenue site where my brother lived, and my partner in crime, helped me navigate Brucie's treatments, doctor updates, and final plans to get him out and home. I truly could not have successfully accomplished the support of my brother's care without Latoya.

My baby brother was dying. He had just been diagnosed with advanced stage pancreatic cancer. Latoya, Janice, and I conferenced immediately with the oncologist to discuss the next steps. Due to his advanced stage and the effect that dialysis was already having on his body, neither surgery nor chemotherapy were options. I mean really, how much more could be asked of him? Dialysis three times a week *and* chemotherapy? We were all in agreement—not going to happen. He would be placed on palliative care with a palliative nurse visiting him at home to monitor his health.

They say ignorance is bliss and I must agree. Brucie knew when he didn't feel well but had no comprehension of the seriousness and implications of his illness. He was happy to be released, getting hugs from his nurses and the doctors. "I will miss this sweet guy. You are so lucky to have each other," and "He is so lucky to have you. I will miss his smile in the mornings," were comments I heard repeatedly. More people appreciating the essence of Bruce.

As his ERCP procedure was unsuccessful, Bruce was transferred to Temple University Hospital, a blessing, where the nurses and doctors not only conversed with me multiple times a day but offered to visit with my brother so we could FaceTime, delighting in his personality and our interactions.

He would eventually need a stent in his bile duct to help with his digestion of food. This was the only procedure agreed upon to ensure he received nourishment. Surgery was successful. It was recommended that he stay overnight, just to be sure, which was different from the original plan to go home that day. Thank goodness, because at 1:00 a.m., the phone call came with news that my brother was in serious trouble. He was bleeding internally —from where was not yet discovered and permission was needed for surgery. The bleed was found and corrected, and Bruce was back in his room after a transfusion by 3:00 a.m. He remained in the ICU for a few days, receiving round-the-clock care for monitoring and then moved to the regular floor for discharge.

A trip to Philadelphia was not planned until the beginning of August to allow Bruce time to settle into a routine of care. Dialysis proved too taxing; so, after speaking with the nephrologist, Janice, Latoya, and I agreed to try two times a week with strict monitoring of his numbers by the dialysis center and his new palliative nurse, Justina. Bruce and Justina bonded quickly so visits were more social than negative while checking his heart, blood pressure, and red blood cell count. Justina and I conferred after each visit so that I was kept abreast of any concerns or recommendations in changes of care.

Although I was isolated and far away, I was never alone. Latoya and Janice were ever present through texts and calls to not just discuss Bruce's care but mine as well. I still marvel at how blessed I was. My brother David and his wife Lisa were wonderful, always available to talk and just as concerned about me as they were about Brucie. In support of my mental health were my husband, children, and nieces, sending photos to make me laugh and always calling to check in. My granddaughters' FaceTime chats and family Zoom meetings kept me sane. My solace was hiking the mountain trails of East Vail, listening to the Killers, dancing with the nymphs in the forests.

My daughter Jerica, of course, knew everything. As a graduate of Temple Medical School, she was acquainted with some of Bruce's attendings and was friends with members of his medical team. Because of this comfort level, Jerica was involved with consults and was encouraged to discuss Bruce's care with his attendings.

She and I had more direct discussions—there was no need for buffering or protecting. We knew the good, the bad, and the ugly even before his diagnosis. How to share the nitty gritty details or what to share without causing confusion and pain was not an easy task for me. The most exhausting part was keeping family informed through texts, phone calls, and FaceTime.

SUNDAY

August 17, 2020

I snuggle with Bruce in his bed, watching the original Star Trek as I have for the past five days, savoring the time as this is our first in-person visit since seeing him at Jerica's medical school graduation a year ago. His journal, my prized possession, has accompanied me on this trip and Bruce has taken great pleasure in continuing to write the names and songs of his favorite albums in it. We Zoom every day with David and FaceTime with Randy, his girls, and Jerica. It's important to me that they still have contact so he will not be forgotten. They lovingly comply no matter the time or day.

"This Down syndrome man is soon to turn fifty-three years old in fourteen days and his big sister is neither mentally nor physically challenged—who would have thought we would have so much in common?" I ask out loud to no one in particular. I lovingly list the comparisons between Brucie and me to my husband, Big Bruce: "Star Trek, mashed potatoes, markers for kidney issues, gum disease, rolling our eyes, our love of dancing and music, singing at the top of our lungs rocking out to our favorite songs (not necessarily the same taste in music), teasing David because it's so easy, and the ability to read and work a room.

I have joined The Transition Network (TTN), a wonderful group of retired professional women, and through this group I have met nine very special ladies of my peer group. We have committed to staying in touch with each other weekly through Zoom and they have been a dear source of comfort. One of those very special ladies named Judi had heard of my brother's illness and offered to have us stay at her summer residence, an apartment across from the Philadelphia Art Museum, as she would remain in Florida due to COVID. She immediately reached out to her friend and neighbor Barbara, both taking us under their wings for the eight-day visit. Talk about a caring community. This care will help when Big Bruce and I meet with the funeral parlor and cemetery administrator this upcoming Friday to arrange for Brucie's final resting place. My brother's death has been on my mind for the last few years as leaving him was imminent, and I worried about him outliving me and being buried alone. My parents purchased a cemetery plot in Trevose, PA, for four—long before my grandparents passed away. As my dad was buried in Florida, we had signed documentation transferring my mother's plot to be buried with Dad. This left two spaces. When I moved to Florida, I had my mother transfer one of those spaces to be used by Bruce. Although I was sad knowing my brother would pass sooner rather than later, I felt that a weight was lifted off my shoulders knowing he would be with his paternal grandparents, the same Bubbie Vera and Zadie Pop who raised me as a young child. He would be in good hands. A beautiful rose casket was chosen along with flowers, white lilies and blue hydrangea, and signed contracts. When we returned to the house, I showed Brucie pictures of the casket and flowers asking him about colors while subtly explaining how they would be used.

"Brucie, when Mom and Dad died, they had a casket, a space to sleep before going to heaven. This is what I like. What do you think?"

"I like this color," he replied, "What about Champion sweatpants?"

Changing the subject, I showed him the white flowers, lilies, he had shown a great fondness for on our walks around the neighborhoods in Voorhees.

"Do you like these?" I asked.

"Yes, yes I do. How about blue?" he suggested. We googled blue funeral flowers on my computer so he could make the final choice. Blue hydrangea was a big hit. I did good.

But for now, I try to imagine as I have so many times before what life might have been had he been born normal. Would we still have been this close? Would I have been a veterinarian having maneuvered successfully through medical school not having had to deal with the guilt of leaving my brothers and then the guilt of Bruce being sent to a group home? Would he be married with children? Would there have been more nieces or nephews for me to love? Would kidney disease have still plagued him or, like me, just left markers? Bruce dozes beside me and I smile thinking back to the beginning of our journey together.

～

CHAPTER 1

Welcome Home: The Implosion Begins

*A*ugust 31, 1967

"HE's MONGOLOID," my father sobbed to my grandparents
downstairs in our living room. "Do you all know what that
means?" he continued choking on tears. I was thirteen
when I overheard this as I lay in bed one night, waking
from a dream that my father was crying. No dream. My
grandparents were crying with him, mumbling, I suppose
soothing words of comfort. I thought to myself, "Mom just
had a baby boy. I have a new brother. What does that
mean, *mongoloid*, other than the people crossing the
Bering Strait I learned about in history?" But I instinctively
knew this was something that was heartbreaking because
those sounds coming from downstairs were not happy
sounds. I couldn't breathe and my stomach wanted to be
sick.

1

The following day I would get to meet my new brother. Dad and I would be going to the hospital to visit Mom and Matthew. I would practice the new name and smile. I was told that Matthew was premature by four weeks, so he must stay for a few more days. David, now the middle child, would not be coming with us; he would be going to school. An alarm went off in my head.

It was morning. David left for school and we left for the hospital. My father still hadn't told me about the baby other than, "We decided to name him Bruce instead of Matthew after your uncle in California." Second alarm in my head. Matthew Brian and Marla Beth were names meticulously chosen and repeated ad nauseam by my mother month after month for eight months of pregnancy —and Bruce was now his name? Was he joking? Between you and me, I prayed for a boy, hating the name Marla Beth. My prayers had been answered, but Bruce with no middle name was the best they could do? Not okay. Still, I said nothing. I just nodded.

At the hospital, I was able to see "Bruce" before I saw my mother. There it was, the heart-wrenching realization of what *mongoloid* is, or should I say the realization of the characteristics. Not only was Bruce scrawny and tiny but his slanted eyes and abnormally long tongue hit me like a punch in the stomach. The hardest thing I have ever done in my life, to date, was to pretend everything was perfect when I visited my mother's hospital room that day. "OH... He's so tiny," was all I could offer, fighting tears. Mom was ecstatic, "Isn't Matthew adorable and the tiniest thing you've ever seen?" Wait, what? Matthew? She didn't know? How could she not know? I didn't know what I didn't know and even I knew. "Yes, Mom. He is the tiniest thing I have ever seen. When are you coming home?"

Ah, this is why David went to school. At the tender age of nine, he was being protected. I guess I didn't need protection at almost thirteen years of age. Hell, always the one standing up to my father's and grandmother's tempers. They must have forgotten I was still a child also.

"I know about the baby," I blurted the minute my father and I walked out of the hospital. "I know and Mom doesn't. How is that possible? Who told you and why doesn't she know?" I was yelling at that point. So angry. But at who? My parents? The doctors? God? Not God. Not yet. Still too focused on my mother's ignorance of the situation. My father's only reply was, "Do you know what this means? How hard this will be? Too hard." Not, "Sorry, honey. This must be scary for you," or, "I was waiting to tell Mom when she is stronger so we could help you and David understand," or even just a hug.

Nothing. I would eventually realize this was the beginning of the end of our parental safety net. We were to become two ships adrift, my parents in one and the three children in the second, the only tie being Bruce, our new handicapped baby.

~

MOM CAME HOME ALONE. Bruce needed more time in the hospital. David and I were called into the master bedroom independent of each other and given the bad news. I was called in after David to be told Bruce would not be coming home. My parents, according to my father, had been declared mentally unfit to care for their handicapped child so he would be placed in Pennhurst State School, an institution in Chester County, Pennsylvania. Stunned into silence, I went straight to my Britannica Encyclopedia to do some research. There, with photos so gut-wrenching to support the abuse and inhuman care, was a naked young child chained to a chair in his excrement. Of all the photos, that picture haunts me today, fifty-three years later. They were sending this helpless newborn to a place I wouldn't send a dog. I brought the encyclopedia to my parent's bedroom. Placing the book in front of my mother, I whispered with my heart in my throat, "I wouldn't walk my dog there and my brother will not be going here." In my mind, the next step was to call my Bubbie Reba. "Hi, Bubbie," I said into the phone trying to hide my pain, "Would you like some company for a few days?"

"*Mamaleh* (a Yiddish nickname for Little Mama), what's wrong? You know I would love to have you, but first, tell me what's wrong." What could I say? *Your daughter has lost her mind? My baby is going to an institution to be abused?* "Nothing," I blurted, "Just need some time away from the grown-ups." After a long sigh she said, "And, what about school?" Her accent thickening as it always did when she was upset. "Bubbie," I started crying. "Mom doesn't want Bruce to come home. They are giving him away. You have to help!"

Even though we were closer to my Bubbie Vera (Dad's

mom), who had raised me and had two bedrooms David and I had been using for years, it was not a very convenient trip to get to her. We would have to travel via three buses into North Philadelphia, which would take us an hour. My Bubbie Reba, on the other hand, lived in the Olney section of Philadelphia near Einstein Hospital. It was a short walk from the bus stop to her apartment. I chose Bubbie Reba because we'd only take two buses to Olney, the W bus (a three-minute walk from our house), and then the Y bus to Olney station. We could even walk to the Y bus on Cottman Avenue if David felt up to the half-mile trek.

I got off the phone too upset to look for suitcases in the garage. How would I manage to get both of us to school? We could miss a few days. That would get my parents to come to their senses. I needed to talk with David about leaving without scaring him. He would be upset but he would listen to me as he always did. The suitcase was gotten and packed for one night. My parents had no idea, locked away together in their bedroom. My dad finally came down to make sure we had eaten dinner and said goodnight. He looked awful. Red eyes, slouched shoulders, defeated. My mother had sent him to check on us. Still not a family talking, planning, and grieving together. We were abandoned for the first time, but not the last.

David and I left in the morning for my grandmother's apartment. There was the love, support, and comfort we had been missing. My Bubbie came through. She had spoken with Bubbie Vera and the four grandparents were going to meet with Mom and Dad to discuss a plan of caring for Bruce. This time, our lack of inclusion was because they realized we were children and, although we were a great source of help, we needed them also.

Bruce came home. It was almost normal. We went to school every day, came home, and had snacks before Hebrew School. For David, Hebrew school was Monday and Wednesday. It was Tuesday night for me. A strange rhythm found its way into our lives. David and I were so excited, the naivety of youth, the lack of feeling hopeless because the world is full of possibilities. A new baby to play with, teach, introduce to our friends. I remember my joy with David, babysitting for him in his playpen and getting an allowance at the age of four and a half, feeding him and watching his smile as he came to recognize me. Now David would know that feeling as well being the big brother.

Bruce as a baby

Zadie Baizer came by bus three days a week like clockwork to help his daughter and baby grandson. If you didn't know, you might miss the cracks; it was an amazing feat as he was never involved with us as babies. He learned to change diapers with those huge safety pins. Pampers were not on Mom's radar just yet. He would give him a bottle, take the stroller for long walks, and—his ultimate favorite activity—sit on the patio in his wife-beater and shorts, rocking Bruce, and listening to his precious Phillies play baseball on the radio. Bubbie Vera filled in the other two days as she had a much longer and tedious schlep with Dad driving her home before dinner. Weekends were for the four of us arranging our schedules to ensure Mom was never alone with Bruce.

Mom was unusually quiet while we were home. Yes, she asked about our days, reminded us about homework, but with no follow-up. No prying about lunch time, who I ate with, friends, after school activities. No checking David's homework knowing he struggled. She was there, but not like before. Like I said, almost normal. One afternoon while changing Bruce's diaper Mom asked nonchalantly, "Lynne, how would you feel if Bruce was gone?" Alarm! Alarm! Danger, Will Robinson!!!

Holy God, what did that mean? How do I answer that? Gone, like *dead* gone? Deep breath. "I would really miss him," was all I could manage. All she said in response was, "Okay." *That was it? Just okay?* There was no follow-up with: "No, we would miss him also. Nothing is wrong with him...Didn't mean to scare you."

This was not okay. I asked David if Mom asked him any strange questions, but he shrugged and said no. He didn't seem to get what was going on and that was its own kind of blessing. At nine, he was so easy, making no demands as the brand-new middle child, only wanting to help. I realize now she was trying to feel me out, give me clues. I was lucky not getting them. A nagging realization set in and as time went on, it became apparent I had been correct. We were abandoned again. It remained that it was my parents against the world, no matter the support of my grandparents or the love and constant help from David and me. The family unit offered no solace nor were their other two children recognized as natural resources of hope. It would not be the last time.

My Zadie Pop, my hero, passed away when I was fifteen. The first parent and grandparent to die. My heart was heavy. My parents and grandmother were bereft upstairs. David, Bruce, and I left downstairs with my other grandparents and family I had never met before. That nagging feeling ever present. The hearse arrived taking my parents, grandmother, and other family to the funeral home. Once again, my Bubbie Reba coming through, securing a separate ride for us and as we were not included with family sitting in the front pew, ensuring we were surrounded by her love and support. I thanked God that David and I had each other, because it was the last time I depended upon my parents for any emotional support.

I did have an issue, though, not just with my mother. Being active in the synagogue youth group was getting harder as my anger about Bruce grew. How could God, my God, allow this to happen to children? I finally told my father I wanted to convert to Christianity because Jesus would never have allowed this. Looking up from the newspaper, he gently replied, "Honey, there is only one God. Call him Eloheinu, Jesus, Allah, George, Sam, or Michael. Tell me what's going on." (I did have to laugh at the thought of God being called George or Michael.) I tried to explain my rage managing to hold back the tears: "How could a God be so cruel? What could any helpless child possibly do to deserve this punishment?"

"We cannot pretend to know what God has in store. You have found your voice. Ask him yourself. It's not like he doesn't know what you are thinking already, so just ask. If you still want to convert, we will not stop you." As a pretty devout Jew, my dad was being cool about this converting issue. For the first time during this ordeal, my father had managed to say the right words to calm me, for which I was so grateful.

That night in bed, I challenged God to a conversation. I was neither polite nor reverent. "You and I have to have a talk. Why was my little brother born with Down syndrome? How could you not know my parents would not handle this well when they are already in denial?" Nothing.

Silence. Well, what did I expect? I did not want to face this rejection and hurt from his lack of acknowledgement. I refused to back down or show weakness as I cried myself to sleep.

In my dream, God answered: "Lynne, of course I knew your parents could not handle this crisis. I am God for goodness' sake." I was sitting in a comfy chair across from this old man. He continued, "They already had issues with David, poor guy. I truly believed that having to deal with a special-needs child, the family would come together. Teaching Bruce would help your parents understand that David needed help and was struggling. I also knew you would be there. So, tell me, haven't you found your voice and risen to the occasion? Didn't you help keep Bruce out of the institution? Haven't you helped David? Your baby brother is a gift to love, cherish, and protect. See how David now has someone to worship him? Someone he can help, being no longer helpless himself? You will grow to become the woman you were meant to be." Once awake, I informed God, "This is not over. I will be back," feeling a sense of serenity that would not last long.

CHAPTER 2

Mission Impossible: From Northeast High School to Penn
State

September 1971-July 1972

ANIMALS. I loved animals. Dogs and horses were my favorites—wild, trained, large, small. I dressed my neighbor's
kittens in doll clothes and walked them in my girlfriend's
stroller. I walked the neighbors' pets just to help. I was
going to be a veterinarian from the moment I walked my
pet pigeon on the Atlantic City Boardwalk at the age of
three. The poor thing hurt its wing and my Zadie Pop
helped me tape the wing and build a coop to keep it safe. I
loved that pigeon. I devoted every morning and evening to
its care. Until one day it flew away, breaking my heart. I
was inconsolable. My grandfather patiently explained how
I had saved this animal and I should be proud he was
healed. "But if he loved me, he would stay," I wailed. "If

you truly love him, you should respect his need to be free."
My Zadie was my hero.

Bruce came and my mission to save animals changed to
saving Bruce and children like him. That way, he could
live a normal life with the family. I had found my voice. I
was confident, jumping into every endeavor headfirst, eyes
wide open without fear of a belly flop. I have since learned
to give some thought prior to jumping. I'm confident, not
stupid. I might waver a time or two, or even three, but
once committed, I'm all in—no stuttering from the start.
That is how I walk. I'm a strider. Head up, shoulders back.
"She knows where she's going" or "That's a woman on a
mission" were comments that whispered, carried on the
breeze created as I passed. I did have a mission now, a very
special mission: becoming the woman I was meant to be.

The Influence over People Begins

October 1971

There were happy milestones along the way, even through the sadness. David had his bar mitzvah. Bruce was four and a half and beyond adorable. We had no way of knowing this would be one of the last family events where we were all living together. Our family loved music, my dog Nippy included. I played the saxophone (my dad's saxophone) with Nippy howling along to "Heart and Soul," "Moonlight Serenade" and "Moon River," and I sang in the high school choir. Favorite music: Motown. David played the clarinet with Mom and Dad singing along as they had both been in their own choirs. Bruce was no exception. He danced and sang to everything. His favorites: Cat Stevens, James Taylor, The Beatles, Rolling Stones, Eric Clapton's "Layla." He put up with Motown only for me.

Mom was a nervous ninny, worked up about seating arrangements and food. The event was at our synagogue, not at home. Never comfortable hosting dinner parties, cooking was not her forte. We had a caterer, so that meant no cooking. We had a party planner, so no last-minute organizational memory lapses. You would think this affair would be a cakewalk. What was there to be nervous about? "Just wait until you are an adult planning for your children," she admonished. "Don't start, Lynne. Don't aggravate your mother," my father added his two cents. David, Bruce, and I locked ourselves in my room and helped each other get ready. Once again, managing nicely without them, or in spite of them.

We were off to the synagogue for an amazing day.

David had a rich tenor voice then—he's a baritone now—and sang flawlessly. Bruce, in awe of his big brother, was mesmerized into silence. Next was the party with a seven-piece band, great food, and lots of dancing. Bruce and I never left the dance floor. After two hours of music, the band, a regular with the synagogue, left the stage for a break. Within five minutes, we heard the drums bang with a unique beat. My little brother had climbed onto the drums and was jamming, singing into the microphone, "In-A-Gadda-Da-Vida." People with Down's are tone deaf, but this was pretty distinct. Well, we joined the jam and so did the band members, middle-aged men in tuxedos playing this psychedelic song. They got back on stage and played around my brother's beat. He stole the show. People who had never met him were falling in love, asking questions about his handicap and wanting to learn about his "specialness." It was like watching those UNICEF ambassadors opening the eyes of the world. My neighbors who had been afraid of him wanted to be included in the limelight, claiming, "We've known Brucie for years, our children grew up with him." I finally had my vindication and revenge, shutting them out like they had done to him. Mean, but worth it. The photo of Bruce on the drums still makes me smile. Today, that would have made YouTube with millions of likes. His charismatic world dominance just beginning.

Bruce on drums

I focused on applying to colleges far enough away to allow for independence, but not so far that I could not make the drive home. I narrowed my search down to those offering courses/degrees in Abnormal Child Psychology as it was called back then. My finds were Beaver College, now called Arcadia University, and Penn State. Although accepted to Beaver, I was so prepared to live in the Castle; I chose Penn State because they offered substantial financial support and a well-established child psychology department.

June 1972

Graduation from Northeast High School was bittersweet. Friends were leaving for Israel before starting college and I was leaving in July for Penn State. There were so many parties that weekend that my friends and I left our own parties, meeting up to party hop everyone else's and eventually coming back to my house. Why my house? Because they needed their "I don't know when I'll get to see you again" hugs from Mr. Adorable who was like a baby brother to all of them having taken their turns babysitting with me.

I began in the summer semester to get a head start on

the program. My father, David, and I left during a torrential rainstorm during the Harrisburg Floods of 1972. Little did we realize the four-hour drive would become seven hours. We had to stop several times to fix my bike that was tied to the roof of the car and detour flooded streets. My father and brother dropped me off with a kiss and hug to turn around for the ride home, afraid to leave my mother any longer. What a way to begin a new experience. My first thought was that I had been abandoned yet again, dumped in front of Pollock Dorm, my new home, to be cared for by my roommates' parents. I know, you're thinking, "What a brat." Not to worry, I came to my senses acknowledging their fourteen-hour ordeal and discomfort at leaving my mother. But you cannot fault me. It was my first time away from home. On top of all that, I was riddled with guilt about leaving my two brothers.

School was postponed for a week due to the floods. Imagine: summer term, 1,000 freshman and graduate students with little supervision. Sleepaway camp could not have been any better. When classes began, my 15 credits (5 classes) consisted of Math, Spanish and Child Psychology 101, 102, and 201. Liberal Arts required math and a foreign language, or I would have taken two more Psych classes. I was on a mission, jumping in headfirst. Seeing no point to the math or Spanish, I focused on two things, having a great time and my Psychology classes. I received my first two failures and deficiency points in my educational career. Undeterred, working at the college bookstore, taking five more classes, writing, taking Spanish 101 again and three child psychology classes, I failed the two classes not worthy of my attention and gained two more deficiency points. Noticing the pattern yet? During my third semester, I was still working at the bookstore when I received a notice from the Bursar's office that my preregistration courses had been denied due to the second time of insufficient funds. That old nagging feeling was back in the pit of my stomach. I must have looked pretty pathetic because my boss—not one to give leave time—taking one look at my face suggested I take the next morning off. "Please take all the time you need," he offered to my surprise.

Insufficient funds, the second time. I had been allowed to complete the second semester basically for free. The problem could not be with the loans as I would have been notified to any changes in status, I believed. There had to be a mistake, a mix up of processing. The nagging was pushing towards panic. I refused to accept the other alternative, the part I may have played in this screw-up. "Breathe. Just breathe," I told myself on the way to the bursar's office. *What's the worst thing that could happen?* I thought, *I would have to reregister and possibly get stuck with all electives? Not the end of the world.*

Mrs. H., the bursar's administrative secretary, knew my family history, having counseled my parents on the FAFSA paperwork and timeline schedule during the summer semester due to a time management issue. That same pathetic face burst into the office straight to Mrs. H.'s desk. To her credit, Mrs. H. ushered me into an empty conference room, "Someone get us a glass of water and call Professor M." In a soothing tone she said, "Now, honey, you just sip some water. Everything will be just fine." I wanted to believe her and not the nagging feeling that procrastination had struck again.

I just hate that nagging feeling, the one that is always right, that settles in the pit of my stomach refusing to lighten up no matter how much denial I choose to seek. After a lengthy conference, the situation was remedied and my parents received an updated timeline. Well, I'd had it. Three semesters of reminders and support from the bursar and my parents were still filing past the deadline. Two embarrassing semesters of begging professors to wave class closures and late enrollment. I was tired of feeling angry, anxious, and guilty, feeling that life was out of my control no matter how much I planned.

Mrs. H. had introduced me to a professor she felt might add extra support for my first time away from home, Professor M. In retrospect, I should have gone to him prior to this visit. He ended up being most influential in my getting preregistered courses after the first glitch this summer.

The guilt was bad enough needing a different kind of help than my mentor could provide, but I could fix anxious and angry with his help. Standing up for Bruce, I had learned to stand up for myself. I had challenged God and now it was time to challenge the State. Having witnessed firsthand what my parents' inability to handle the FAFSA deadlines cost my mental state, I convinced him to help me declare myself financially independent and even meet with my father to help him understand. A date had been scheduled for our meeting with Professor M. and the governor's office and Dad drove up the day before for what he thought was just a financial meeting.

Dad and Professor M. hit it off immediately. They shared the same love of history, music, and a dry sense of humor partly at my expense. I didn't care. I was too nervous about how we would break the news about why Dad was really invited there. "So, Professor," my father asked with a smirk, "My daughter made no bones about how really upset she is with us, using language a truck driver would be embarrassed to hear. What is it you really want?" The professor told my dad what was up. That was it. Easypeasy. A solution to take the weight off of my dad's shoulders. How could he not agree?

The three of us met with representatives from the Pennsylvania governor's office in Harrisburg and the rest, as they say, is history. I was no longer beholden to my parents for filing tax returns or sending in paperwork.

With finagling and lots of pleading, I managed to salvage three out of the five classes and only take two electives. Knowing my established pattern, you can correctly assume more failures and deficiency points, but at least I got straight 4.0s in all of my upper-level psychology courses.

My first two terms of college were complete. I was skating through Psychology, working at the bookstore, and paying my own way through college. I felt on top of the world. Right after gaining my independence, I came home for a surprise visit. It felt like a need to see both of my brothers. I couldn't tell you why, but that nagging feeling had returned. A friend had driven a few of us into town and dropped me off. The house was dark and empty. Strange. David should have been home from school and Mom outside waiting for Bruce's daycare bus. With a rock in the pit of my stomach, I called my Bubbie Reba, knowing I was in for a rude awakening to my best laid plans. "Hey, Bub. I'm home. Have any idea where everyone is?" Silence. Then, I heard a deep sigh. "Bub, what's going on?" Again, no answer. "Bye, Bub, I'm calling Aunt Clara."

My Aunt Clara was Bub's oldest sister and my role model for living single. Her motto: "A woman does not need a man to feel complete." Taking me shopping in New York, eating at upscale restaurants, and never pulling any punches when giving her opinion, Aunt Clara would level with me if something was not kosher.

"Hi, Aunt Clara. How are you?"

"Your parents placed your brother in a group home. Surprise. I am so sorry. I told them it was wrong. Oh, welcome home."

She was never one to mince words, but this one time would have been welcomed. I couldn't say anything, so I hung up, defeated. I knew it the minute I walked in the house. I'd felt something off the last time I talked to my parents. Bruce wasn't available to come to the phone and David was out. My brothers never missed an opportunity to talk to me as I rarely called home on a whim, let alone show up.

Waiting for everyone to come home, everyone but Bruce, I reminded myself to give myself time to process the news. I should have been shocked, furious. No one told me or asked me how I would feel. Well, let's be honest, of course no one would ask me. I was the force that brought him home, made my parents take responsibility, and then I left. Would *I* have asked me? Hell no. My parents had waited for me to get out of Dodge and bam, mission accomplished. Once accepted to the group home with Ken-Crest, Bruce became a ward of the state. My parents had signed their guardianship over to them.

What gave me the right to condemn them for their decision? To them, I had left to live my own life, to follow my own path and dreams. They had been deserted, still unable to cope with the "hardship" of a mentally challenged child, believing they were unfit as my father continued to remind us. I realized his new involvement in so many organizations was not his way of running away from the situation (that's what the many visits to Penn State accomplished) but was for networking with a support group of people in the know who could politically help him with Bruce. Being honest with myself, I did not actually harbor resentment for this decision. After all, I was not a parent and had no idea how I would act in this same situation. I gave no grief when they came home. I fought them once; I would not fight them again. Obviously, they hadn't totally lost their minds.

I had missed being able to say goodbye to Bruce and felt guilty for having left both brothers. I turned eighteen years old that December and I was finally legally independent. I could now file to become Bruce's legal guardian. However, he was now a ward of the state so that option no longer existed. Carl and Nancy, Bruce's group home parents, were a gift from whatever being I chose to believe in at the moment. Bruce was enrolled in school, learning to read and write with their support at home as certified teachers. Education had finally advanced, understanding that even Down Syndrome children could be educated, and should not simply be relegated to Life Skills classrooms. Unfortunately, this would not last. Bruce was also on a swim team with the Wahoos, running, and participating in Special Olympics and medaling. Each weekend that I came home for a visit, I was trying to come home more often, with guilt as a driving force, I brought Bruce home as well. My heart smiled watching him flourish. He climbed into bed with me early on those weekend mornings. We read together, snuggling. He would say, "I know dis letter, I can read dis. Listen to me, listen to me!" Those mornings were soothing to my soul as my life at school was racing to disaster. (More on that later.)

My father became involved with KenCrest by sitting on the board, attending Bruce's Individual Learning Plan meetings, and participating in group home activities. Bruce had been with Carl and Nancy for almost a year now, and he had come home for Thanksgiving. While serving dinner, Bruce was making strange signs with his fingers and giggling at David. He crawled under the table to whisper in my ear and signed again pointing to Mom. The light dawned like watching Helen Keller with Anne Sullivan in *The Miracle Worker*. No one seemed to get what was going on other than me. "If you'll excuse us, I'm taking Bruce to the bathroom." Once there, Bruce signed again. "Are you signing, like sign language signing?" I asked, amazed. He nodded, signing, "This is *messy*, and

21

this is *love*. Nancy showed us so we talk to Tommy." Nancy and Carl taught the boys sign language so Tommy, one of Bruce's group home mates and best friend, would have an easier time communicating. Tommy struggled with speech as do many Down's individuals. This was my first introduction into sign language other than for the deaf. Sign language, how amazing. As the educational system itself was just waking up to special needs potential, these two individuals had no doubt their "boys" could be fluent in a second language. Laughing, I asked, "Why did you sign *messy* and point to Mommy?"

"She has gravy all over her shirt like Tommy when we eat meatball sketty. Nancy says Tommy is messy and we laugh." Heading back to the dinner table, we decided to share with David. The three of us signed through the rest of dinner, laughing.

My family had been blessed and I wondered if my parents appreciated the gift. My lesson learned? Sometimes you don't get what you want, but you do get what is needed. Bruce was in great hands.

$\sim$

CHAPTER 3

Let the Reckoning Begin

all 1973

I WAS A NATURAL, destined to become the world's utmost expert, the Einstein of Abnormal Child Psychology, until summoned one afternoon to the Dean of Psychology's office at the end of the second semester of my sophomore year. Bragging to my friends of my upcoming meeting, I was pleasantly surprised to see my mentor and my father in the conference room as I entered. "Oh, so nice to have you both here. I knew I was getting some kind of award." This was immediately followed by the dean clearing his throat, "It seems we have a serious issue here, young lady." Busted and not even sure why, I sank into the closest chair as he continued, "How is it possible you have managed to take upper-level psychology courses as a new sophomore? Some of these are reserved for graduate students. On top of that, you are one deficiency point away from being expelled from this university." Taking a long pause, he continued, "Well, what have you to say for yourself?" I looked at my father and felt awful for him. No matter how many planned or surprise visits he had made, gifts he had sent for Thanksgiving and Hanukkah (even remembering my birthday), and phone calls, he was totally unprepared to face the fact that the one person he completely believed had the wherewithal to survive—no, not just to survive, but to rise above with the strength of Hercules over our family's implosion—was faking it and no one had any idea...until now.

There wasn't anything I could say without hurting my father. What was I going to say? *Well, Dad, I was on a mission to save Bruce so you and Mom wouldn't need to give him away. Oh, wait, been there done that?* Or *Making Bruce normal would help Mom wake up and be a better mom to David?* Or, even better: *Once I graduate and become a famous child psychologist, Zadie Baizer would have to apologize for telling my mother terrible stories about me made up by Aunt Mary.*

My Aunt Mary is my grandfather's sister and grandmother to my cousin Renee who was also attending Penn State. Of course, knowing my mom was upset by these stories only added to my guilt in leaving and the anger that she believed them. I chalked this up to her losing her mind. Fortunately, my mentor had inferred some of this mess from our many talks and visits. He was an ongoing gift I was grateful to have step in, once again.

"You do realize that Lynne has managed a 4.0 in each of these courses proving she belongs in this field. She and I will develop a plan to deal with the deficiency points," my mentor jumped to my defense.

Sounded good to me. I mean really, how difficult could it be to make up math, Spanish, and writing courses? I had four years of Spanish in high school. I took trigonometry, calculus, and had excelled in language arts classes. My mentor's plan was not to be. The dean's plan: no more psychology. Not just classes; the major, period. Booted out of the department permanently. Not even offered probation if I pulled up my grades. "She's lucky we're even keeping her in this institution" were the last words offered by the dean in a huff before throwing us out of his office.

I had to give my father credit. He turned to us and said, "That guy scared the living you-know-what out of me. Lynnie, I cannot believe how you held your own." He went on, "Well, you're smart. You can do whatever you want. Just pick a new major. You love art, music, and history. Do you know how lucky you are?" The fact is, I did know how lucky I was. Although devastated about psychology, I wasn't devastated about the turn my life would have to take. It was like a weight had been lifted from my shoulders. What else did I want? Bruce's birth had been the impetus to run away, gain my strength and legal independence for guardianship, and flourish in psychology, which was a life path I would have never taken otherwise. Was this the sign to go back to my original plan of veterinary school? Did I have the fortitude to begin from scratch? Could I handle science courses for pre-med and make up those deficiency points? I felt defeated before I even started. I thought back to my father's words. I could do anything I wanted. I did love history, art, and the fashion of certain eras—especially the shoes.

New major, one that accepted most of my courses and would not force me to repeat Spanish, Fashion, and Retail Merchandising. I will admit now something I knew but have never revealed to the public, it was the easiest transition I could have chosen. Penn State's program required a semester of apprenticeship called Co-Op, which supplied a list of approved retail establishments to which you would apply and hope to be "hired." In retrospect, this was great practice for creating a resume and skills in interviewing. By comparison, Drexel University's program helped their students secure their apprenticeship, but those who struggled resented being abandoned.

I was lucky to be accepted for the summer semester by Strawbridge & Clothier, which was well respected within Philadelphia retail circles. Having to live at home for the first time in three years would prove challenging, but I would be spending quality time with my brothers and be home for Bruce's eighth birthday, a decent trade off.

I graduated from Penn State in February of 1976 with a 3.5 grade point average and honors. David and my parents made the trip without Bruce. This was the first family event in which he did not participate. My mother insisted that the four-hour ride was too long for him to manage at the age of eight. That nagging feeling reared its ugly head for a brief moment.

I GOT ENGAGED and went to work for Strawbridge & Clothier as an Assistant Buyer in women's sportswear. Dealing with consumers, not much different than children, I soon learned how beneficial those psychology courses would be thanks to my baby brother.

David was next to graduate Northeast High School in June of 1976. Again, Bruce, now almost nine, was greeting everyone at the door and was even more charming than ever before. David's friends were just as much in love with him as mine had been. David was just as devoted, including Bruce in everything appropriate when he visited on weekends. Everyone we knew, knew about our baby brother, having met him in person or heard stories. He was special and we were special by association and devotion.

. . .

My WEDDING DAY was finally here with quite a few bumps along the way. What a whirlwind this year this had been. The house had been given a facelift for my bridal shower, complete with my mother and me butting heads over wedding arrangements and problems already brewing between my fiancé and me. David had gotten Bruce on Friday night so he could spend the weekend. Mom was a raving lunatic about the house not being ready for guests and last-minute wedding plan mistakes. The wedding ceremony and reception would be held in our synagogue, our home *away* from home. My dad was frazzled not knowing how to help her. Once again, I couldn't figure out the tummel, but remembering the admonishing words from David's bar mitzvah, I held my tongue. Not an easy feat. Obviously having already planned a huge affair in the past had still not prepared her for this.

History does repeat itself. Packing a suitcase for Bruce and me, David drove us to the synagogue. His personality was so different from mine. My parents' lunacy and fighting washing over him, he had no issue going back and dealing with them. Bruce and I helped each other get ready. Zipping up my dress. Brushing my hair. My girlfriend Susan met us there to help with my makeup.

Bruce was so taken that he spent the next half hour trying to convince everyone he met to come back to the bride's suite to see his beautiful sister. It didn't matter whether he knew these people or not; to him, I was a vision to behold. "Lynnie, you look so beautiful," he breathed. He was just as adorable in his tuxedo at the age of almost nine as he had been at the age of four. My wedding colors were red, white, and blue for the Bicentennial. My bridesmaids were in blue gowns carrying bouquets of red roses with white baby's breath, and the groom's men were in baby blue tuxedos with one red rose and baby's breath pinned to their lapel. My fiancé wore a light brown tuxedo with chocolate brown trim. Before I could react, Bruce—Mr. How to Make Friends and Influence People—blurted out loudly, "Brown, brown doesn't go with blue, you don't match." No need for me to speak, the point was driven home by a nine-year-old with more sense of style and propriety than the grown-ups.

The ceremony took place without further snags and the reception and food were a success. The seven-piece band, the same band from my brother's bar mitzvah, left the stage for their fifteen-minute break. Well, history continues to repeat as my little brother—you guessed it—made his way toward the drums. This time it was Aerosmith's "Dream On," which the band did not know, so they let Bruce drum and sing alone through the entire break. My college friends, many only knowing both my brothers from shared stories, were quite taken with his personality and charm. They rushed to the stage to clap and cheer. I expected to see Bic lighters held up like you do at a rock concert. My brother the rock star thanked all of them for coming. Just as before, new people were conquered, wanting to spend time with him and learn more about his story. My original major in child psychology was being recognized.

CHAPTER 4

Time Marches On: Losing Track of Time

I must admit to less of an involvement during the next few years. I had a demanding job in retail and an unhappy marriage along with a growing resentment toward my parents. They held on to wasted emotions, which made them unproductive, but they were there nonetheless. It seemed the more I was involved, the less they stepped up. I always saw Bruce when he was home for the weekends, but without my insistence on his inclusion, my parents were slacking off, finding it inconvenient to work him into their schedule. Bruce moved five times during his tenure with KenCrest, his first move due to Carl and Nancy leaving the "family." But, have no fear, he had three consistent caretakers who remained with him until the end: Cedric, Ms. Lee, and his second true love Janice. They would soon come to participate in many family gatherings, becoming my extended family and sharing Bruce's milestones along the way.

. . .

I HAD BEEN MARRIED four years, living in my own home on Levick Street across from Tarken Playground. I was near my parents and soon Bruce would be a bar mitzvah. Bar mitzvah? How the hell did that happen? Thirteen years had flown by.

David and I were in college. I was at Temple Ambler working on my MBA and David was close to graduation from Gynedd Mercy. We were aware of the positive changes in Special Education Standards having had friends in the field, so learning that our synagogue—with its huge congregation and day school—had no one capable of preparing Bruce for his special day was incredulous. He would be taught and bar mitzvahed at a reform synagogue in Elkins Park, PA, called Kenneth Israel because they were more "equipped" to handle him. Imagine your whole family being members of an institution for fifteen years—my father on the board of Men's Club, Mom involved in Sisterhood, me active in youth group, USY, and overnight camp—but needing to go elsewhere because your congregation was not equipped.

"There isn't one congregant in this synagogue certified in Special Education who can work out a plan with us? No tape could be made so that Bruce could play it and learn the prayers by heart as they do for other kids? He knows words to a bazillion songs and can sign fluently. You don't think we can get him to learn this?" I was speechless. Well, after this tirade I was speechless. I wanted to meet with the rabbi. The rabbi who had bar mitzvahed David. The same rabbi who had married me. I could not accept his resignation at not wanting to be involved with this latest and even more special *simcha* (blessing). Sensing my parents' discomfort, I did not go to the rabbi. This was for them to handle and if they didn't want to make waves in their synagogue, it wasn't for me to make them uncomfortable. Of course, making waves is how change comes about and can be accomplished with grace and respect. Bruce would manage to do that on his own.

I did insist upon two things: the rabbi's attendance on that day and a celebration. While over my parent's house for dinner one Sunday with David and his significant other, we were teasing Bruce about his part and singing along with him for practice. "Is the reception right after the bar mitzvah or on Sunday?" David asked my dad nonchalantly. I had been bugging him to ask this for weeks because my parents changed the subject or got testy whenever I broached the subject. He insisted I was imagining things, but finally agreed to ask. "There is no party!" Dad yelled looking at me. "He's having a service with family. Isn't that enough?" Like they were doing me a great favor. "No, not enough. Not even close. "You get more excited about my dogs learning a new trick than about your own son's accomplishments." I was done. I left.

IN RETROSPECT, my anger was more frustration and heartache for my parents who dearly loved but could not appreciate Bruce. They could only feel guilt and responsibility for his shortcomings, being constantly reminded of his handicap. Janice, Ms. Lee, Cedric, the other caregivers in his group homes, David, and I on the other hand reveled in all of Bruce's wins, taking great pleasure in watching him get there and sharing this joy with as many people as possible.

Suffice it to say, Bruce did have his bar mitzvah in September of 1980. I cried through the entire service, *kvelling* (the Yiddish word for beaming with pride) with David by my side. Even my father-in-law who, like Mikey hated everything, was impressed. Our rabbi was present, and a lovely luncheon for family and friends followed, held in my home. This was good. This was right. Overcome by the service, witnessing the love and support for Bruce by Kenneth Israel's rabbi and teachers, KenCrest caretakers, and our friends, my rabbi realized what he and his congregation were missing. Change was on the way. Bruce continued his influence on world domination with grace and respect. My heart still smiles at this memory, a framed picture of Bruce with his first girlfriend on a shelf as a reminder. David and I still appreciate how lucky we are to have had this gift.

MARCH 5, 1982

ANOTHER MOVE BROUGHT the group to the Germantown area of Philadelphia. By March 5, 1982, Bruce was a freshman in high school and a brand-new uncle at the tender age of fourteen years, really still a child himself. "I'm a mommy and you are an uncle. Meet your nephew, Randy." I gently tried to place Randy into Bruce's arms after the ceremony known as a *bris*. For the first time, my sweet adoring brother was not happy with me. He was agitated, refusing to even look at Randy. Revelation: Bruce hadn't lived with me for ten years and had not had me full time since I left for college. He was jealous of this baby, my baby. I was reminded again of our strong bond, our souls the same as I promised him that he was and will always be my number one. This satisfied him and the love fest between those two was always a beautiful thing to behold.

Working to keep that promise, Randy and I attended as many of Bruce's Special Olympics races as possible while I was on maternity leave. Bruce learned to change diapers, give bottles, and walk Randy in the carriage.

JUNE 1989

BRUCE WAS GRADUATING Germantown High School. Please, let's not forget senior prom. A white tuxedo jacket for my brother, just because he could. Being comfortable on the dance floor, Bruce literally danced the night away making John Travolta and the Bee Gees proud with his Saturday Night Dance Fever moves, so I had been told. If David's bar mitzvah, my wedding, and bowling alley dance parties were any indication of his prowess, I had to believe the stories of prom.

My career, problematic marriage, separation, divorce, and baby had kept me busy and less active in Bruce's life. (I am not excusing this or asking for understanding, just offering information). We never missed a family dinner when Bruce was home, his birthday, or having him at my home for the Jewish holidays and Thanksgiving. But I do not recall visiting any of his group homes or keeping track of regularly scheduled visits home as I had previously done. These gaps in time and missed information would become more apparent in the coming years.

I hadn't been to a high school graduation since David's twelve years ago. My parents, Randy, and I rode together so we would only have to take one car. The school tried to honor their special Life Skills students by including them while keeping them separate. Bruce did not disappoint, strutting across the stage to the podium when his name was announced, shaking hands appropriately with the principal and then everyone else in his vicinity before strutting back to his seat waving to the crowd. And that crowd cheered letting him know he was appreciated. How President Reagan or any of our future presidents did not appoint him ambassador to God-knows-where or even Secretary of State I will never know. I was so proud, crying and laughing while waiting in the wings to congratulate my brother. Bruce would now begin his career at Ken-Crest's work facility—that we fondly called the workshop— getting paid by the pieces he packed in boxes. So many milestones reached. Twenty-one years since we brought this very special gift home from the hospital.

JUNE 1990

. . .

PHILADELPHIA MAGAZINE WAS the original Match.com. My girlfriends answered an ad of the man who would become my husband, stepfather to Randy, and staunch supporter of my little brother.

Funny enough, I ended up marrying that man and he also happened to be named Bruce. We moved from Philadelphia to Voorhees, New Jersey. I did get to see a glimpse of Brucie's old self at my wedding, charming the crowd with his dance moves, but not having a drum to play because we had a DJ instead of a band. Big Bruce, as my new husband would be called, and Little Bruce would begin their own unique bromance, both Bruces looking forward to family dinners where they could watch Little Bruce's beloved Eagles or Phillies on TV. Little Bruce understood nothing about football and wasn't able to actually see the TV since he refused to wear his glasses, but he still loved sitting with his Big Bruce and talking sports. Unfortunately, life is not a bed of roses and into every life rain must fall. Although corny phrases, they were sad but true. Down syndrome individuals are prone to serious health issues. Of course, with Bruce being no ordinary individual, he would be diagnosed with a serious disease not due to his Down's. After years of testing, tried and failed medication regiments, special diet plans, weight gain, weight loss, and a general change in his love of life, in 1991 at the age of twenty-four, Bruce was finally diagnosed with kidney failure.

A strict diet and dialysis three days a week was started for him. Obviously, being mentally challenged had not been enough. Yet, Bruce's sweet disposition prevailed, even with the pain of a shunt in his arm and painful dialysis sessions until his salt and urine levels stabilized. The only noticeable change was that he no longer enjoyed swimming and sports as he once had. It seemed his energy level was gone. Time for a new conversation with the man/woman upstairs. That would have to wait as I had just given birth to a baby girl, Jerica, and my parents were now forced to deal with dialysis schedules, medications, and an uncompromising diet plan during home visits which were becoming less frequent. All three needed extra support from David and me. So that's where my energy was focused. My goal: lessen the burden on my parents and ensure those home visits.

BY THIS TIME all family holiday dinners and many Sunday dinners were held at my home, allowing my mother off the hook in adhering to Bruce's strict diet and creating meals to help him feel included. I love to cook and playing with recipes and ingredients is a fun challenge for me. Polenta mashed with butter and milk was a delicious, healthier substitute for mashed potatoes. Stuffing, loved by all members of the family, not just Bruce, became a second staple. No-salt chicken soup was used as now my parents needed to watch their diets.

Those on dialysis must be mindful of their potassium, salt, and dairy intake among other things. This meant that Bruce would have to give up tomatoes and potatoes, his two favorite foods. As a little boy, he would steal the tomatoes Mom left to ripen on the windowsill, eating them like one eats an apple. No menu was complete without Bruce asking for garlic mashed potatoes. Kosher salami and hotdogs were off the menu due to high sodium and nitrates. I found frozen organic vegetables, unheard of back then for my parents, and cauliflower rice with garlic and milk we could make as fake potatoes. Macaroni and cheese would become a new love. Of course, the amount of cheese had to be monitored. Medications became a mainstay. Supplements for the B12 he would get from milk. The phosphorus binders he took to limit phosphorus build up, also gotten from dairy, in the kidneys would eventually lead to weakened bones and loss of his teeth because phosphorus from dairy strengthens teeth and bones. It makes sense he would not have the same energy, but I was still learning all about this disease.

Bruce's involvement in Special Olympics and sports in general continued to dwindle while waiting for his final diagnosis of kidney disease. He lost his love of swimming and running. The energy needed for these sports was just not there. It was so sad as he had earned many a gold medal for running in Special Olympics. However, one sport he was willing to learn was soccer. Why? Randy played soccer and during Sunday visits to my home, along with my parents, everyone would attend Randy's games.

I use the term *learn* loosely. Bruce's education began with volleys back and forth in the street in front of our house. Randy would gently kick the ball to his uncle, who finally figured out he needed to kick the ball back, not pick it up and throw it. We would listen to their conversation from the driveway. "Okay, Uncle Bruce. I will kick the ball and you kick it back, like this. No, no. Don't catch it. Just kick it back, like football."

"Football?" Brucie would ask. "This is not a football," Randy clarified. Even at a young age, Randy had great patience and respect for Bruce's unique learning and physical capabilities, never getting frustrated with the repetition of instructions and coaxing his uncle who often did get frustrated. "Oh, come on," Bruce would shake his head, his face crinkling up. "I can't do this." And he would walk away, Randy chasing him down to convince him back. The two had their own special bond. Though Bruce loved his nieces Arielle, Robyn, and Jerica, and his great-nieces, Randy's daughters Maddie and Emily, his number one fan was Randy, whose comfort level with him was amazing. While growing up and now during Christmas visits back up north, watching them debate music, best artists, and Rock & Roll Hall of Fame nominees acknowledges that I did a good job making sure my brother would be remembered as an integral part of this family, stamped on their hearts forever.

We set up trash cans, bicycles, and our large planters as borders so the ball would stay in bounds during play, allowing the space to grow along with Bruce's developing ability. Eventually, my father, Big Bruce, and I created a goal post so a "real" game could be played, with my father as permanent goalie and Big Bruce and me taking turns as rotating teammate or opposing goalie. My mother, cheerleader for both sides, received Brucie's infamous dirty looks if she wasn't cheering for his side. "Oh no, you cheat!" Brucie would stalk off our court shaking his head and hand once someone other than Randy or himself scored. He would allow us to cajole him back to the game as we laughed and ran after him. He enjoyed this game just as much as the soccer game. By the time Jerica joined her soccer team, Brucie was a pro, insisting either Randy or Jerica be on his team. When asked why he wanted the kids, we were told, "They know how to play." If Big Bruce and I scored, Brucie would then insist on both so he could beat us, still claiming we cheated and loving us to cajole him back. We had a soccer ball, baseball, and football at the house in a bag with his name, hung next to Randy and then Jerica's bags for whenever and whatever he wanted to play. Their sports becoming Bruce's sports. His enjoyment of playing with "his kids," as he liked to call them. Wonderful to watch.

My only regret was not being able to teach him how to ride a bike. He could never master the balance no matter how much we supported his weight or modeled what to do. We ended up finally donating the small girl's twenty-inch bike with training wheels to Goodwill. Of course, in true Brucie fashion, once the small bike was gone, he decided he needed to learn how to ride Randy's 24-inch bike. I am five-feet-two-inches tall and weighed, at that time, ninety-eight pounds. Brucie, four-foot-ten inches, weighed one hundred and twenty pounds. Guess who he wanted to hold him as he tried to get on the bike? The scene was as ridiculous as you can imagine. Nonetheless, I had the bike leaned against me, trying to get Bruce to stand on the curb and swing his leg over the bar. When you look up the word *klutz*, bear this picture in mind. By the third time of falling over with my brother on top of me, with the family laughing too hard to help, I gave up. We couldn't get Bruce or David to peddle a tricycle when they were younger, let alone now, so I finally conceded defeat. Not an easy task for me.

After a year, Bruce was put on the donor list for a kidney transplant. David and I learned of this once a kidney donor had already been found. I appreciate my parents trying to protect us, knowing David and I would gladly have given a kidney or two if it meant life would be made easier for Bruce; my parents' explanation of our wasting a kidney would have been typical. I did mind not being given the option at the time because he might have gotten the kidney sooner.

It was around this time, being a parent myself now with one child much older than the other (Randy is nine and a half years older than Jerica) that I saw what my parents had completely missed about David and me all those years ago and still now. Just how much of a positive influence and resource that older siblings can be. We never saw Bruce as a burden, especially David. If we were Christian, David would be slated for sainthood. Whereas I would huff and roll my eyes, eventually doing what was asked. My parents would just look like deer in the headlights, and

David would just say "Yeah, sure, no problem," and do the thing that was needed. He was consistent and dependable, making the rest of our reactions seem selfish and petty, which they were. I watched Randy's influence over Jerica, his pleasure in teaching her new things, accepting whatever she did and delighting in her learning as we had done with Bruce.

The transplant was a success and Bruce's body's acceptance almost immediate. Having no other health issues, he healed quickly and was ecstatic to be able to eat all of his favorite foods once again. His energy levels improved giving him back his zest for life.

They say God does not give anyone more of a burden than they can handle. We will agree to disagree, because although Bruce's new kidney was healthy, he developed Cryptococcus and almost died. He spent weeks in the hospital on antibiotics receiving blood transfusions.

A particular visit during one of these transfusions has stayed with me throughout his life and other illnesses, to remind me to always make sure that if he ever returned to a hospital, he was never left alone. Jerica was with me. She had come to cheer up her Uncle Bruce. Walking down the hall on the way to his room, I explained to a two-year-old Jerica what she could expect to see: tubes to machines, a bag for urine as he had a catheter, and normal hospital stuff. What I saw sent chills down my spine and bile up my throat as I tried to shield Jerica from a mess. Blood all over the sheets shooting out of his arm and my brother spilling on the floor. Bruce wailing, "Help me! Can you help me?" unable to press the button for the nurses. Running out of the room screaming for help, with Jerica's head pressed to my shoulder, I was hysterical to say the least. I went to the nurses' station demanding to speak with the doctor, head of the hospital and God only knows who else. My parents were in the family waiting room—waiting for what, I still don't know—until I got them. Nurses came running to Bruce's room with the crash cart, obviously only a misunderstanding of a code blue could rouse them. If I hadn't been so upset, I might have appreciated the irony.

Chaos ensued as my brother had not coded and was very much alive albeit bleeding to death. Finally, the tube was replaced in my brother's arm, new blood for a transfusion on the way along with demands for an explanation from my father. The heads of Nephrology and Nursing met with us to discuss next steps and avoid the threat of a lawsuit not just from us but also from KenCrest. Bruce's records were sent to Temple University Hospital and he never set foot in that hospital again. Lesson learned. We must advocate for those who cannot against those who will not. Unfortunately, I have learned that the care of mentally challenged individuals has not greatly improved, their only hope being a strong advocate.

Bruce finally beat the infection and healed but the medications used caused his system to ultimately reject the once-accepted kidney. You would think he would be devastated, but Bruce was so happy to be well and out of that hospital. He remained his sweet self even though he would have to return to dialysis and the strict diet. What a source of inspiration and heartache, my own ever-sweet, naïve Don Quixote.

FEBRUARY 25, 1995

TIME MARCHED ON. Bruce readjusted to dialysis as we looked forward to Randy's bar mitzvah. March Madness was the theme. Randy, the ever-devoted nephew, called his uncle to light his own memory candle. Music truly soothes the savage beast and Bruce once again entertained the masses with his dance moves, visiting with Randy's friends, charming the girls and asking them to dance.

DECEMBER 1997

NEXT, it was David's first born Arielle's bat mitzvah. It was a family road trip to Florida including Bruce and my parents on the same flight and staying next door to each other at the hotel. David had moved there a year ago, so we were all excited to visit. I don't know who was more fun to watch during the flight, Randy with Bruce, Randy with Jerica, Bruce with Jerica, or my parents with their grandchildren, spending the two-and-a-half-hour flight seat hopping. Janice helped secure a dialysis appointment for Bruce convenient to our hotel and the synagogue, so once we landed, we were free to visit and enjoy summer in December. David and Bruce spent those hours with each other as if they had never been apart. Arielle made us proud Saturday morning with her, Jerica, and me winning the dance competition at the party Saturday afternoon. We spent the night at David's home to enjoy an intimate family dinner after he returned from dialysis with Bruce.

We were in for a very rude awakening. Dialysis, we thought, was a four-hour session with Bruce on a machine listening to music while having his system flushed. Nothing more, nothing less. Yes, we knew the stress it had on his body. Yes, we acknowledged his patience, sitting through four hours with nothing to do, but never having been involved, we had no idea about the havoc if done incorrectly. It could either take too much salt or not enough fluid. Being a new center with no history, just records from Philadelphia, too much fluid and salt were taken, leaving Bruce in excruciating pain, doubled over crying.

David's wife Nadine, a nurse, called her hospital for advice. I called the dialysis center. Between the two of us, we learned that Bruce needed to be fed salt mixed with the tiniest bit of water. Can you imagine having to eat salt? I love salt—that is my equivalent to chocolate candy—and I was nauseated having to feed this to Bruce, who of course was in too much pain to cooperate. Hours passed with everyone helping to distract Bruce, eating dinner in shifts. The children were amazing, telling jokes while lying on the floor to get Bruce to laugh before we could get him comfortable. We regrouped, having survived the evening together with a major blip, an inconvenience. Not the end of the world. Now feeling better, Bruce helped plan the next day's events with everyone but my parents. If there had been any hope of including Bruce in more road trips with them, it ended that evening.

CHAPTER 5

Changing Tide: New Tests in Fortitude

*D*uring this time, I left Strawbridge to move from the department store environment into chain stores to gain more experience with merchandising, displays, and selling more than buying. Randy's father and I finally separated, and I now had a new set of challenges as a single mom living in an apartment and working nights and weekends. Paley Day Care Center became our new home away from home for daycare and weekend extracurricular activities.

I did return to department store life, Bloomingdale's in Willow Grove, only working one night a week and every third weekend. I enjoyed working the floor, but missed the control of what merchandise would actually be sold and, who could turn down an opportunity to work for Bloomingdale's? I would be an Assistant Buyer in women's sportswear, traveling back and forth to New York twice a month and merchandising the floor. A win-win situation. Eventually I became a Department Manager of all women's accessories, turning down the position of Buyer in New York. As a single mother, traveling back and forth to New York on a daily basis was unreasonably demanding and relocating to New York was not an option. I would not separate Randy from his father and grandparents. Buyers with whom I worked became close friends, affording me the opportunity to take the lead in many deals with vendors while staying in New York, purchasing what was needed for my local store. I have many fond memories of times spent in Soho.

Sundays that I worked were special for Randy, who was three years old by this time. He spent most of the day with my Division Head, walking the floors, wearing a walkie-talkie and lunching in Bloomingdale's infamous restaurant. When with me, we brought merchandise to the floor from receiving and created unique displays within the glass casing. Randy had a natural talent for arranging by color scheme or what he perceived to "go together." While Randy was being supervised, I spent time learning to dress mannequins with help from the display department. Why would I need to learn this having our own in-house professional display department? I wanted control over the merchandise used on those mannequins surrounding my accessory department. I was a hands-on Department Manager who observed customers, was willing to spend time on the sales floor with customers and my staff, and filled in merchandise, which taught me what sold and what women wanted. They wanted ensembles, outfits that go together, bottoms with matching tops, with matching accessories, already created for them to see. I sold accessories, scarves, gloves, slouch socks, headbands, pantyhose, scrunchies, swatch watches, athletic clothing, and sunglasses to name a few. My mannequins could help increase sales through cross merchandising and they did.

I was enjoying my life, having great success at work,

involved with Paley, being President of the PTA, having a wonderful boyfriend, but the divorce proceedings, kindergarten, and extended hours at Paley were taking its toll on Randy. I had spent twelve years immersed in the world of fashion. I made wonderful connections and friendships with designers and owned a great deal of those designers' clothes as gifts and hundreds of pairs of shoes. It was time for a change.

While a new Department Manager, I noticed my younger part-time staff (high school and college students) were unable to count back change or add and subtract in their heads, needing the cash register and using their fingers while checking in merchandise. They were unaware of current events, social issues, taxes taken out on their pay checks. Too many mistakes were made, and registers were short while cashing out at the end of the night. I met with Human Resources asking if we could offer a basic arithmetic/life class. "Only if you are willing to teach this," was their response. My response to Bloomingdale's was "I will if you make this a mandatory part of training." They did. So became the start of my educational career. Ironic how life works. My aunt Clara wanted me to be a teacher and I told her, "Not in a million years." Here I was, teaching young adults and enjoying the experience.

I had discussed making a change during my many meetings and conversations with the Director of Paley, Helen Victor Turk, a wise woman with a gigantic heart.

"You're a natural leader. You're wonderful with our parents and the kids love you. Why not teaching?"

"Really?" I answered sarcastically, rolling my eyes with a deep sigh. (Remind you of anyone?) Laughing, she went on. "I know you enjoy working with the high school and college age young adults, throwing in social issues while working on math skills." *Hm*, I thought, *I did enjoy those*

evenings teaching and found the age group stimulating.
"Okay, I'll look into this."

Within two weeks, I was enrolled in Beaver College's Master of Education Program in Secondary Education. It was now called Arcadia University, where I had been accepted as an undergraduate. Many of my undergraduate child psychology courses were accepted for transfer and graduate federal government financial aid was available. The program had flexible hours in the evening, weekends, or both. This was meant to be as everything fell into place so easily. It aligned with God's plan for me to become the woman I was meant to be.

Brucie loved to study with me during our family visits together. My parents would entertain Randy while Bruce and I "studied" upstairs. He would look at picture books and I would read my textbooks. The School District of Philadelphia was offering emergency certification to elementary school teachers willing to teach in the inner-city schools who had completed five education courses with a grade point of 3.0. This meant I could be hired, have my teaching experience count toward the student teaching requirement, and earn a living. I would have to change to elementary education, giving up my desire to teach political science. The compromise was a kindergarten through eighth grade certification instead of high school. In 1989, I began my career as a sixth-grade teacher with the School District of Philadelphia. Strawberry Mansion Middle/Senior High School would be my new home. My courses and experiences with Brucie made the transition into education, although extremely challenging, successful. Helen had been correct. I knew what was needed to help struggling learners be successful: patience, creativity, and a sense of humor. In June of 1991, I graduated from Beaver College with a teaching certification and master's in education, while pregnant with my daughter.

In the fourteen years I spent in the classroom teaching first through ninth grade, I had one Down syndrome student in one of my fourth-grade classrooms, and I knew my purpose was to support inclusive classrooms. No matter how stressful or painful teaching could be, this vocation was truly where I belonged. I fell in love with each class, that specific grade being my favorite at the time. I enjoyed learning strategies at professional developments, rushing back to the classroom so my students could benefit. Please, don't get me wrong; there were many times I cried, "What the hell have I gotten myself into?" and struggled with parent conferences, angry students, and losing my cool. But the next day, one of those children would give me a hug, or tell me I was cool, or ask me for help, or read a sentence successfully, and all was right with the world. When the opportunity to support new teachers was presented due to the large turnover rate in Philadelphia inner-city schools, I was encouraged by the district to apply for a position that would assist them. I was torn. I loved being in the classroom, watching those young minds work and think, allowing my own curiosity to bring them along with me towards discovery.

In 2003, I became a "New Teacher Coach" along with forty other very talented educators. Now, I would help support 20–30 classrooms of students modeling best practices, positive classroom management, and neighborhood involvement, the goal to retain newer teachers before they became frustrated and left, leaving classrooms dependent upon rotating substitute teachers. Seven years, hundreds of teachers, and thousands of students later, I became an administrator, returning back to our own classroom with my dear friend Sheila for certification. I had seen enough good teachers struggle due to poor school management and principals being the roadblock to creative teaching. Educational bureaucracies are enough of a roadblock, in my opinion. Principals should be hands-on bulldozers, helping their teachers and staff plow through that bureaucracy.

LIFE HAD QUIETED DOWN, and milestones continued as part of life. The youngest member of the clan, Jerica, would be a bat mitzvah. Fortunately, Jerica's bat mitzvah was local so the only family needing to travel were David and his girls and Big Bruce's family from New York, consisting of my sister-in-law Cindy and her children, Uncle Al, and Aunt Lorraine.

It was finally the big day. In support of her uncle's inclusion in the service, Bruce and his niece Robyn, David's younger daughter, were given the honor of opening and closing the ark. Mr. Personality, ever the gentleman, escorted Robyn holding her arm up to the *bema* and then the ark. On their way down, he shook everyone's hand, strutting back to his seat, never failing to entertain.

Then, a huge change. Randy moved to Florida having made a commitment to Laurie, his longtime, long-distance girlfriend, who we loved immediately. Jerica drove down to help her brother with the move—she was sad, but moving to New Orleans herself to attend Tulane University. The farewell dinner to both children was filled with excitement. I rose to make a toast; after all, I was their mother. Not to be outdone, and standing with his glass raised, Uncle Bruce cleared his throat.

"Ahem, ahem."

"Listen to me. I would like to have some toast."

BRUCE COULD HAVE PLEDGED allegiance to the flag at that moment because no one was listening. We were all laughing and repeating, "I would like to have some toast." The more we repeated this, the harder we laughed. Randy gave his uncle the biggest hug, "I love you buddy!!!" Twenty years later, we still laugh at this until we cry. Poor Brucie; he was not handling empty nest syndrome as well as Big Bruce and me. He was lonely for Jerica and Randy.

OCTOBER 10, 2010

DAVID AND LISA'S WEDDING, (10-10-10), was on a beautiful fall day in Philadelphia. My father, Big Bruce, and Little Bruce all looked dapper in their tuxedos. My brother's was a tad different as he would be sharing the honor of Best Man with David's best friend, Brenda. "So Brucie," I asked nonchalantly while pinning his flower to his lapel, taking responsibility for Bruce as everyone else was either getting ready or too nervous, "I hear you are the best man."

"Yes, I am."

"So," I continued, "As best man, what do you do?" Bruce proceeded to roll his eyes and sighed deeply at such a ridiculous question, like, "Why are you bothering me with such trivia?" He then lay his head on my shoulder and fake cried saying, "I don't know." Laughing, I asked, "What did David tell you?"

"I don't know. Where is Benda?"

"Would you like to talk with Brenda? Then we can figure this out."

"Yes, please." And all at once he was back to his happy self, strutting down the lobby shouting, "Big Bruce, we are going to meet Brenda. You can come too." Brenda had known us for years and was very comfortable with Bruce. After hugs and friendly formalities, I turned to her and said, "Brenda, Brucie has something to ask" I winked.

"Yes, Brucie. Please go ahead. Ask."

I whispered a few hints into his ear. "I would like to know what this means," he said. She looked at me confused. A few more whispered hints. "Best man, what does that mean?" Smiling, she took his hand and explained what they would do together and how excited she was to be with him.

David outdid himself in choosing a best friend. As they chatted, I was dismissed with the wave of Bruce's hand "Oh, Lynnie, you can go now." Chuckling and feeling comfortable that Bruce was in good hands, I returned to my husband to help pin his flower to his lapel and visit with Randy and Laurie who had flown up from Florida to attend their uncle's wedding, sharing the story of Bruce and Brenda.

Bruce and Brenda were adorable together, sharing their responsibility and having us all laughing with their antics and banter. During the reception, our table was filled with family, including Janice and my cousin Polly who I had not seen in years. Remember my cousin Renee, granddaughter to my aunt Mary, my Zadie Baizer's sister? You know, the aunt who told my mother terrible stories about me at college where Renee also attended? Polly is Renee's mother. Small world. Well, Polly who I have always liked and liked even more now, could not get over how youthful I looked and acted compared to Renee, who was wrinkled and grey. I just smiled inwardly appreciating my just desserts. Awful, petty, I know—but enjoyed nonetheless. It was a wonderful day filled with laughter and dancing, lots of dancing. Janice and I dragged my brother into every line dance, especially the hora.

Lisa and her family were wonderful with Bruce as he had been included in all of their family festivities during Lisa and David's visits during Christmas.

. . .

RANDY MARRIED Laurie two weeks later. We all flew to Florida for the most amazing experience at Vizcaya. The garden ceremony was beautiful like being in a fairy tale. My husband was a groomsman, and my daughter was a bridesmaid; they walked down the aisle together. During the reception, overlooking a sunset which was breathtaking, my husband made his desire to be a grandfather well known by exclaiming, "Bring on the grandchildren!" This moment was immortalized on video for all to see and hear. To the opposite extreme, their Zadie, my father, was telling them to take their time. Not to rush. To enjoy life together. Me, I was basking in their joy of finding each other and knowing I had a fun place, South Beach on the bay, to visit. I regret to this day Bruce's lack of attendance. As mother of the groom, I would not have had the ability to take full responsibility for Bruce's care as I normally did, and no one else volunteered for the job. But this was important. I should have insisted.

Big Bruce and I had discussed retirement in passing, now adding Florida as a potential landing point, but nothing concrete. We were still young, Jerica was in college, and my parents and brother lived in Philadelphia, joining us for dinner almost every Sunday. Big Bruce would bartend. Little Bruce would cook with me in the kitchen and we would always share a snack before dinner was served. I would send trays of food home with my parents and a doggie bag back with Bruce. Where were we really going to go?

MARCH 2012

. . .

53

FAST FORWARD. "Hi mom. Is Bruce with you?" my son asked on the phone, "And, are you sitting down?" I knew what was coming as I had suspected something during their Christmas visit this past December. Laurie wasn't drinking. The annual friends' Christmas party traditionally hosted by Anthony was in need of a new, temporary home this year. We were delighted to host this year's celebration, with beer pong set up in the garage, roaring fires in our always neglected living room fireplace, our beloved family room fireplace, and oh-so-much food strategically placed to enable continuous small groups socializing throughout the house. Food preparation was shared by Randy, Laurie, and me. Big Bruce was thrilled to be bartending for this group we had watched grow up and no longer got to see. While Bruce, Randy, and I either drank a glass of wine or a martini during food prep, Laurie nursed her first and only glass of wine. To quote my mother while watching David eat his peas, "Your pile seems to be growing the longer you sit." Laurie was also wearing her tops untucked, unusual for her with a tiny great body.

Even Brucie noticed something astray during home visits and bowling. This particular bowling night, Laurie—the ever-pleasant planner and bowler—was just not herself. "Laurie, listen to me. Are you okay?" Brucie, the concerned big brother-in-law, asked with his arm around her shoulder. She was more quiet than usual and my brother, so sensitive to my moods and facial expressions, picked up on the unusual vibes. "I'm fine, Bruce. Just tired." Not satisfied, "Lynnie, listen to me," my brother instructed, "What is wrong with Laurie?" and pulling me over to her, "Laurie, you talk to Lynne. You know she is Randy's mother." He proceeded to give each of us a bear hug because in his mind everything would be okay like it was when he called me for help. "Go ahead," he said waving his hand, "Talk." All we could do was laugh, marvel at his intuitiveness, and the simplicity of his solution. Everything really was fine. "See, told ya," he says with a smile, strutting down the lane bowling ball in hand to take his turn.

Then, we were brought back to the future, hearing, "Guys, we're pregnant!" I smiled responding, "I'm so happy for you both, honey. I guess this explains Christmas."

"Yes," Laurie chimed in, "We knew then but didn't want to jinx the superstition of waiting three full months to make sure everything is okay." Turning to my husband, "Well, dear, they listened to you and my dad. A year to enjoy each other, and then, bring on the grandchildren, as requested." Blushing and gushing he took over the conversation with Randy by asking a million questions, impossible to answer, about the new baby.

August 7, 2012

MADALINE BLAKE TORBAN entered the world. We were grandparents, my parents now great grandparents, Brucie a great uncle. I wondered how he would handle his nephew/little brother having a baby of his own. We would find out in a few months.

That Christmas visit was so special. Maddie was four months old and ours for ten days of full-time grand-parenting. Having a grandchild long distant was surreal, but not now. Brucie, thrilled to see Randy and Laurie, smiled at Maddie, tickled her belly, and cooed and made silly faces. He was basically as underwhelmed as he had been with Randy as a baby. "Here, Lynne, take the baby. Randy, how about we listen to the Rolling Stones?" he suggested while walking Randy into the dining room to listen to the group on my laptop.

I got a phone call the next day from Janice. "Hi, Lynne.

Brucie tells me he has a new baby girl Maddie and that she is so cute." We laughed. Obviously, she had made a bigger impression on him than he had let on. After dropping Bruce back off that evening, he proceeded to boast to everyone about his new baby. When prompted for more information, he acknowledged it was Randy's baby. By the second visit with us, Brucie was holding Maddie and singing songs to her, delighting in her cooing back to him. "See? She knows the words."

FOLLOWING the pregnancy announcement phone call, my husband began lamenting our long-distance relationships with our children. That summer while vacationing at our timeshare on Singer Island as we had for the past eleven years, visiting David and Arielle, and Robyn, my husband shopped real estate. Palm Beach Gardens down the highway and across from the island was up and coming. We had watched its development over the years while grocery shopping, eating at our favorite Italian restaurant, sharing a cigar and my favorite—a 10-year Tawny Port—in PGA Commons. New townhomes were for sale and they were the perfect distance from Juno Beach and Jupiter, with the added benefit of being a forty-minute drive to my parents and David and an hour and fifteen-minute drive to Miami Beach. Just to humor him, we went to see some sample homes. Caught up in his excitement to move closer to the "kids," we bought a townhouse in Paloma, convincing him a single home was too much house as we got older, having already compromised on a two-story home over a ranch style home as agreed upon in early retirement discussions. We told no one as per my request. Voicing this purchase we had made in Florida out loud—not my first or even my hundredth choice to settle—made the decision to leave Jerica and my brother a little too final for my mental wellbeing. If we didn't say it, and no one heard it, it wasn't real. We would be leasing with plans to move roughly seven years later. My plan was to rent it, pay off the mortgage, use the rental money for travel, and call it a day. I had seven years to plan the un-move to Florida.

Zadie Pop (left), Bruce, Zadie Baizer (right)

Bruce with his girlfriend at a dance (age 13)

Robyn, Jerica, Arielle, Randy, Bruce, and my
mom and dad (from left to right)

Bruce playing soccer with "his kids"

David (left) and Bruce at my home for
Passover, 1996

Me and Bruce, Passover 1997

Us, Passover 2001

Best man at David's wedding, 2010

Bruce on our deck before we moved to the
Vista

Me and Bruce in front of his 50th birthday-
wall

The two of us at his 50th birthday bash

Bruce enjoying his niece Jerica

Proud uncle Bruce with Jerica at Temple's
Medical School Graduation

Bruce with his two sisters, Janice and me, in
his bedroom during our first visit in August
2020

Bruce and me in January, enjoying the cold
while walking the Vista grounds

CHAPTER 6

Time All to Myself: Five Years of Love

*M*y parents had moved to Florida, leaving Bruce and me to be the only family left here in the north. What a blessing it was as Bruce spent every other Sunday with us. The round trip began with me picking him up early Sunday after grocery shopping and taking him back late in the evening after dinner and dessert.

We spent our time working on little projects as agreed upon on his IEP. Some Sundays we rolled coins to encourage his learning to differentiate among quarters, nickels, dimes and pennies. Bruce had to then organize them into piles. Remembering their worth had been a challenge and was frustrating for him. As he would not be shopping on his own any time soon and someone else would deal with the money, causing him stress seemed silly.

So, we focused on the piles and then put them in the rolls to help with dexterity. It was something he could do successfully before I pushed him beyond that comfort zone. He must count how many he has placed into the piles first, which was also a challenge, but one he was willing to take. After many times of forgetting, I had taught him to move them by tens and keep track of them by writing them down so he could go on from there. With practice, he wrote the 10 he had counted, then 20, then 30, and finally had reached his goal of counting 40 nickels for a roll equal to $2.00. He just put them in the roll and talked to us about whatever he wanted. He loved sitting on the floor with us as we had our "family meeting," his words. Coins got rotated when we had enough so if he had done nickels, next would be quarters or dimes. When there were not enough coins to roll, we did laundry. Bruce learned how to measure detergent, line up the arrow to the appropriate setting, and recognize the letters of the words on the machines.

When the school budgets were cut, reading programs for mentally challenged students changed. Bruce was put into Life Skills classes and reading became a secondary focus. He still loved reading letters and asking what they spell. I had him read me the letters of the settings, say the word, and then find what word matched the setting we needed. He had even learned the correct measurement for the detergent. When the washer finished, we moved the clothes into the dryer and found that setting the same way. I had learned that folding clothes was not his forte, but for me, he always tried to be neat. His favorite part of this operation: putting the clothes away. Why? He loved going through our closets and drawers, checking out our clothes and shoes. "Lynne, listen to me. Listen, I would like to try that shirt," or, "Yeah, I need those sneakers." Being a clothes and sneaker hound himself, he was always on the lookout for something we had that he might want. Just for the record, Bruce had so many clothes that they were in labeled crates in the basement of his group home. He could open his own sneaker store offering a variety of styles and colors. We tried to be creative, sometimes going to the movies or bowling, but spending time at home together was always what we preferred as it afforded us the opportunity to talk and share family time. When the weather was comfortable, Bruce loved going for the two-block walk to our lake in the development. He was not one to choose to walk when he could be driven, so this was quite a pleasant shock and a challenge for me—if you remember, me being the power strider that I am. Bruce moved in minus speed, looking everywhere but where he was actually walking and talking at the speed I walked. Although I am an expert at deciphering his messages, even I had him repeat himself occasionally. He rolled his eyes, something else we have in common, took a deep breath and said, "Listen to me."

"I am listening, you are talking too fast. Take a deep breath and try again." Eventually I got it.

This is how I feel walking with my husband, who is not the strider I am unless pushed by an emergency decided in his own head, but definitely a faster walker than my brother. Walking from the car to the farmers' market in Vail, one of our many favorite activities we shared on Sundays, had been more of a chore and less fun for me this summer. As he insisted on holding my hand, our pace had to match even before we merged into the crowds of the market. Need I elaborate any further? Just imagine how this conversation must have gone. Before that painful conversation, I tried giving hints, physical hints, gentle tugs, walking just a few paces ahead to bring him along to a compromised pace, because once we entered the actual market grounds of the wall of shoppers and meanderers, I would completely lose the battle of movement. "In death I will move faster than most of these people," I grumbled. Whether entertaining Lucifer in my reserved suite for five or at the pearly gates with God, I'm a planner. Can't I be an optimist as well? I will move, bend, twitch, or float faster than any of these people in front of me. Hence my urgency to pick up the pace in getting to the market and when we finally left the market, my hints went unheeded, my hand a captive as therefore am I.

Now, imagine me walking with Bruce in minus speed mode—not an easy feat. "Move your feet, Brucie," I chanted. This had become our new mantra together.

"Lynne, how about we take a walk?"

"Okay, but what will you do?"

"Move my feet."

Of course, now that he'd discovered the joy of walking, he also wanted to walk our greyhound, Brenda. Brenda is the smallest of our greyhounds, only sixty-two pounds, not a champion racer like the others, hence the name Brenda, and content to walk at a slower pace. But even she grappled with the lack of speed, sighing deeply, looking at me as if to say, "OMG, really?!" when Bruce got her leash for the walk. They had both learned to compromise. We ended up having to leave him behind by half a block which did make me nervous as Bruce would talk to anything and anyone, not paying attention when crossing the street. He was very understanding and had learned that he must wait at the corner where he could still see us upon our return to him. Brenda had learned that this was a shorter walk, only taking us to the next corner where we turned to come back. Then we hung out on the bench by the lake, feeding the ducks, which they both loved, listening to music on my phone.

Along with "long walks" and hanging at the lake, Brucie also enjoyed, to my astonishment, visiting the bookstore, Barnes and Noble. We had discovered his love of coffee while visiting Mom in the hospital all those months, so coffee was not a novelty, but reading at a book-store for hours was another story.

A recent routine blood test had uncovered high sugar and cholesterol levels which, quite frankly, really ticked me off. For someone who consciously managed both of our diets, ran, paddled on a dragon boat three times a week, lifted weights, and participated in Pilates weekly, any tests with less than stellar results were unconscionable to me. Something had to be done, but the question was, what?

During one of our Sunday visits, I asked my brother to run some errands with me. "Sure, where are we going?" he said. Not wanting to confuse him with too many details, "To the bookstore for some health cookbooks," I explained. "OOHH, cooking, Yes, I'd like those books." Laughing, we left for Barnes and Noble not far from the house. Once there, I guided him to a large table filled with books. "Star Trek! Lynnie, Lynnie! Star Trek!" He shouted with excitement for all to hear. Sure enough, he held up a *Star Trek* book, the original, one of his favorite television shows. "Correct. How did you know, honey?" I asked knowing he could not read and curious as to how he knew. He shook his head, hand on his forehead. The obligatory eye roll and deep sigh one does when dealing with the fee-bleminded. "Lynne, listen to me," pointing to the cover. "That says," and he proceeded to spell, "S-T-A-R T-R-E-K, Star Trek—and that is the enterprise." He had memorized the words having watched the show so often.

"Stay here and look at your book while I check these cookbooks," I had instructed while becoming immersed in two *Whole 30* books trying to discern the differences, for-getting the time and him. "So, Brucie. Are you ready to go?" No response. Looking up, Bruce was nowhere in sight. Not panicked but a tad concerned, I asked the people around the table if they had noticed where the young man standing with me had gone. Pointing to the couches, sure enough, there was my brother, one leg crossed over the other in the coffee/lounge area reading his book. I walk over, not entirely pleased with this, but before I could say anything, Bruce looked up and said, "Lynnie, how about we get coffee and you can sit and read. Go ahead. If you have trouble, I can help. You get the coffee. I want milk and sugar." My turn to roll my eyes, shake my head, and sigh. It was impossible to stay annoyed. However, he did need to acknowledge my concern at his walking away.

"Brucie, I am a little annoyed with you."

"Why? What I do?" his eyes wide with innocence. I am not David, so I just fixed him with a look. "Why do you think I might be upset with you?" That was the clincher as he did not like having me upset. "I walked away." I nodded my head. "When you walked away, what could you have done so I would have known where you were?"

"I don't know." I continued my look.

Looking down, he grinned, "I could tell you."

"Yes. Let's practice what you will tell me next time."

Barnes and Noble became our new home away from home, visiting so often that the ladies placed our order upon seeing us.

"Hi, Bruce! You can come get your coffee whenever you are ready."

Instead of the china cups, our coffee was poured in to-go cups so Bruce could take responsibility for getting our order while flirting with his new fan club. This was one of the many special things I would miss when we moved.

Once we were back home having finished our coffee visit, chores, reading, rolling coins, and eating a snack, Bruce and I settled in to listen to his favorite music on an old laptop I had designated as his. Bruce had a journal we kept at my house where he practiced his writing and more reading. Writing is contagious, so I either write poetry or thoughts about teaching and work on Sudoku puzzles. He dated the page to include the month, day, and year. He then wrote the titles of albums and two of the songs he loved from that album. We then drew. Actually, I drew. "Lynne, can you help me?" he asked with this pathetic face, and then we colored the page. He got such pleasure returning to pages and reading the letters to me, triumphant when he recognized words. This never failed to make me laugh and make my heart happy for him. To ensure Bruce's inclusion with family, Jerica joined us on as many Sundays as her schedule allowed, Thanksgiving, and all Jewish holiday dinners. Randy, Laurie, Maddie, and Emily stayed with us on their northern visits during Christmas, sharing many activities with their Uncle Bruce.

I had learned that Bruce would ask me or the members of his group home for albums by their color, not their title, so we never knew what he wanted. "Bruce, sing me one of the songs," we asked with no guarantee of success. I had gotten phone calls from them asking for my help. The solution: this journal. Along with Brucie's singing, having the artist, color, and songs of each album written down in one place really helped us decipher the album he wanted to listen to.

We also connected with my parents and David, calling whenever Brucie was with me. David spoke with Bruce on a regular basis (he was always the devoted older brother), but I wanted to make sure that we visited as siblings and that David was given the real story, not the Bruce version with creative embellishments. For example, if we asked him, "Bruce, what did you have for lunch today?" Bruce's version: "Well, I had a double cheeseburger with ketchup and mustard, french fries, and a Pepsi from McDonald's. It was so good." True version: Bruce only eats chicken sandwiches, and cannot have ketchup, french fries, or Pepsi due to his kidney issues. Or he would start with something like, "David, my leg is hurting." David would empathize,

"Oh, Brucie. I'm so sorry. What happened?" Bruce's version of the story: "I got pushed at work and fell down the stairs." There were no stairs at the workshop, neither was he pushed. When I gave him one of my looks, *his* looks, he snickered and then told the true version. I've never been able to derive the pleasure he got from this routine other than watching my reaction. Bruce loved talking to our parents, who rarely called him. "Let's call Mom and Dad," he would always say. It was only a short phone visit, but he still missed them.

SEPTEMBER 11, 2015

MY PARENTS DID GO on enjoying life, going on vacations with Bruce and all of the grandchildren, traveling on their own cruises, and taking trips to Disney World.

Years later as an educator, I would come to understand my parents' lack of resiliency. They moved through life, but for all intents and purposes, they had not conquered life. Life had conquered them. This was fine until a serious situation threatened their fragility. It's what I see in my students when they hurt but cannot reach out for help. They act out instead. Sometimes we need to be alone to internalize our pain, but then that inner voice nags at you to get with it, breathe, and go. That inner voice was missing. They struggled with my divorce (Mom more than Dad), standing up to my ex-husband when they disagreed with his behavior, moving to Florida, having to unpack their new home, choosing to live with David and Lisa for almost a month, and ultimately coping with my father's diagnosis of pancreatic cancer.

. . .

DAD DIED ONLY fifteen months after moving there. Having not visited all that time, that December, my mother decided to come up north with Randy, Laurie and the girls for Christmas. What a fiasco. They no sooner landed and while walking to the car, Mom fell, having refused to bring her walker on this trip. Big Bruce and I had planned that evening to meet Jerica's boyfriend's family, heading to Reading, Pennsylvania, for their Christmas Celebration. Randy, only visiting during Christmas to see his father's family, was having friends over our house to begin the annual whirlwind of catching up.

Mom complained of pain, took some Tylenol and was content to just sit, nothing unusual to her normal daily routine at home. Randy and Laurie insisted we keep our plans, so off we went with mild trepidation for the two-hour car ride looking forward to seeing Jerica. Our visit lasted exactly thirty minutes. We were able to meet family, drink a toast to our children, play with Brenda (she really was Jerica's dog no matter how devoted she was to me), have a few bites of food before getting the infamous phone call.

"Hi, mom." It was Randy. "Don't panic." I never panic. "Bub is in the hospital." She had broken her hip and femur unbeknownst to us as she continued to the car after we helped her up earlier that day. We left immediately to meet Randy at the hospital. Talking to him on the drive home in a snow shower it seemed Mom's pain had worsened, and he and his friend needed to carry her to the bathroom. His friend, a doctor, advised going to the emergency room. Fortunately, the hospital was only five minutes from our home, so the ambulance ride and drive were not long. I felt awful leaving my children to deal with this, but Randy, her devoted grandson, just laughed it off. That Sunday was a Bruce day and when I told him that Mom was here, before I could tell him where here actually was, his excitement at seeing her was overwhelming, especially after hearing she was in the hospital. "Mom's here? Oh good. Where's dad? What happened to dad? The hospital—we have to bring a present." I marvel at his ability and openness to love even though they never visited and barely called. First, we stopped home so he could see Randy, Laurie, Maddie and Emily before heading to the hospital, him fretting about what to get mom. Ditching me at the front entrance, seeing the gift shop, Bruce headed right over to the woman behind the register taking matters into his own hands.

"I'm looking for a present for my mother."

"How lovely," she responded, "What would you like?"

"How about flowers? Lynne, come over here." As instructed, I paid for the flowers, borrowing a left-behind vase as they had none, returning it the next day with one from home. I learned that day how much Bruce loved fresh flowers. I knew he liked my plants as he helped with watering inside and gardening outside, but not flowers.

One of my favorite conversations between mother and son was during our second visit at the hospital, cup of coffee in one hand, sitting on the bed, legs crossed, with his other hand on Mom's leg. "So, Mom, what happened to Dad?"

"Bruce," I interjected, "We have talked about this." Dad had just passed, and Bruce only knew he was sick. David insisted upon telling him, but I knew Bruce could not grasp the concept of death and Dad no longer being physically here. Hence the question "What happened to Dad?" Instinctively he knew if Dad wasn't with Mom something must be wrong. He and I talked about death; bugs die, plants die, people go to heaven. And as Bruce called my parents faithfully and heard my father's voice on the phone when asked to leave a message, of course he was confused. Or so I thought. Bruce gave me such a look, if I hadn't recognized it as one of my own, I would have dug a hole to hide instead of laughing with Mom.

"Mom, listen to me. Dad, he was your husband, right?"

"Yes, Bruce he was my husband."

"And you loved him very, much right?"

"Yes, I loved him very much."

"Why don't you tell me about him, you'll feel better."

I found this so endearing my eyes filled with tears. Such pure simplicity of thought and feeling. This man with the mind of a child, really, and a heart of gold trying to make his mother feel better about Dad while in the hospital.

Bruce spent every one of his Sunday visits in the hospital and eventually the physical therapy facility for hours until Mom was released to my care at the end of March before I could fly her back home in April. I really can't settle on what he loved the most, chatting while making cups of coffee on the Keurig machine, "This coffee is so good. Now Lynnie, listen to me, how about we talk about Dad" "Brucie, talking about Dad makes Mom sad."

"Why? I love my dad. I like to talk about him."

"Okay," I relented, "but first ask Mom what she wants to talk about." We enter and wham, "Hi Mom, what do you want to talk about. How about we talk about Dad?" I did tell him to ask, which he did. I never specified waiting for her to answer.

We had to visit the gift shop each time for a gift because God forbid we should walk in empty handed. Do the math: fourteen visits, fourteen presents. He was costing me a fortune.

"Bruce, you are costing me a fortune."

"I'll pay, I have money."

"Really, where's your wallet?"

"I don't know"

"Is it in your room in your drawer?"

"Yes, it is." This was the same conversation each time. During each visit, he was learning to play the card game Fish, watching TV, and flirting with the nurses. He asked about Mom each time I picked him up. He was excited to spend the day with her and was very sad when she finally left. They may have never come to see him, or called him as they should, but he was ever devoted until my mom's death in July of 2019.

AUGUST 2017

WHILE GOING through family photos and planning for Bruce's 50th Birthday, I was reminded that my parents, while they were flawed as most human parents, were exceptional grandparents. Mom was so into becoming a grandmother, not caring what she was called, when I became pregnant. She researched natural childbirth, Lamaze, and breastfeeding strategies just to support me. Dad was determined to be a Zadie. While collecting unemployment, every Wednesday, my dad would come over to watch Randy so I would not have to schlep him on those cold March mornings. "Dad, he should sleep through this nap. I'll see you in two hours," I told him before leaving. Randy never fussed during this nap, but without fail, I would always come home to hear footsteps upstairs and my father saying, "It's okay, *tatelleh*, (little boy in Yiddish) Zadie's here, don't worry." I'd quietly walk upstairs to see grandson and grandfather cheek to cheek, while walking the floor. My father upon spotting me would say, "He was fussing. I didn't want him to cry and not see you." After a few weeks of this I told him, "Randy looks so comfortable and happy hearing his Zadie talk to him." My father was in heaven. How do I know? My mother called as soon as he got home, laughing. "You made your father's day. He's down in the office calling his friends to tell them how good it feels to be a Zadie."

They were involved with each of their grandchildren individually and all together, taking them on weekend trips with campouts in the living room. For vacations, they rented a van so that everyone could be included, even Uncle Bruce. They finally realized Bruce needed to be included in his nephew's and his nieces' lives, not just with me for Sunday and holiday dinners. These photos I had found showed Bruce in so many stages of growing up, or growing old as I liked to tease him.

Besides having a look that could bring a grown man to tears and facial expressions that showed exact feelings, Bruce and I shared the traits of rolling our eyes and sighing with deep exasperation. The trait that all three siblings had in common, however, was having finicky eating habits. Bruce was more set in his ways than truly finicky, David was close to impossible, and I was the most flexible but still discriminating. Neither one of my brothers would eat fish. David has been won over with shrimp—his limit; Bruce, not so much. He called me during one dinnertime to say, "Lynnie, listen to me. I don't like fish."

"Okay, honey. Who can I talk to?" Handing over the phone to either Stephen or Ms. Lee, I heard him in the background, "See, talk to my sister." These were some of the funniest conversations about Bruce's eating habits and how I managed to get him to eat fish at my house. Inevitably they would make him something else. I always made the same suggestion, "Chop up the fish and mix it with macaroni and cheese."

How did I manage to get Brucie to eat fish? Elementary. My dear Watson, pure manipulation. Four years of upper-level psychology classes had to offer some strategies. Big Bruce, Jerica, Randy, and I love fish. My children learned to read the nutritional facts on the back label of food products at a young age while grocery shopping, even taking responsibility for finding items on the shopping list to keep them occupied. My mother had done the same, hoping that learning about healthy eating would convince David and me to eat our fish, liver, and vegetables. We did learn to read those facts—high sodium was bad, vitamins A and C were good, and that was it. In our home, good for you usually meant bad tasting. In later years, I realized my distastes for liver, fish, and most vegetables were because of how they had been cooked.

Fortunately, my children liked vegetables. Randy was so easy, loving almost any food, and Jerica was impossible about anything else. She had grown to have an eclectic taste in food, surpassing even her father and brother. So, on holidays like Rosh Hashanah. when I experimented with stuffed flounder or baked salmon with orange and pineapple sauce, and Passover, for which I would make horseradish crusted tilapia (using homemade seasoned cake meal instead of breadcrumbs), I would also make either a pot roast, brisket, rib roast, or some chicken for Jerica and my brothers. As Brucie always helped me in the kitchen, I would tell him about the fish first, waiting for his face to crumble. "That was an ugly face, and *this fish is NOT for you*," I would emphasize. He would shrug it off, "Okay." However, sitting with the family and our guests and watching the fish platter continuously pass him by was another story. He would sneak over to Big Bruce and point to the fish platter not saying a word in fear of me hearing him. Instinctively, he knew after that ugly face that hell would freeze over before I would give him any of that fish. His brother-in-law was the safer bet.

To the day of his death, I had only raised my voice to my brother once. Yet, he was committed to never doing anything that might cause me grief. I think my first greyhound, Bazooka, is the only other being who has loved me like that. I read a quote once that said losing someone you love is hard, but losing someone who unconditionally loves you is devastating. I must concur. All these years and two dogs later, I still miss that dog.

So Big Bruce would ask, "Bruce, would you like some?" Bruce's response with his forefinger and thumb pressed together, "Just a little bit" would become one of the family's favorite Bruceisms repeated by us, our children, and now our grandchildren with a fond smile or giggles. Of course, Brucie loved the fish, returning to his group home that night bragging how he had fish and it was "so good," another Bruceism. Despite this, he made us repeat the ritual each time fish was served. Of course, the house knew Bruce liked fish—but it was my fish, not theirs.

Randy, an exceptional cook, cooks for his family and friends, creating sauces and dishes regularly. On holidays, he loves to make fish and either meat or chicken, like his mother. His Uncle Bruce would be proud.

"Brucie's 50th Birthday!" Janice and I exclaimed together over the phone. Bruce was always ready to celebrate this date, a date he remembered well and loved with the wonderment of a child, still. "Lynne," Bruce explained his wishes during a phone call, "How about the Rolling Stones red album?"

"Okay, honey. I will get you Sunday and we can go shopping."

This had become our ritual for birthdays. We would go to a small store in the neighborhood selling new and used CDs, tapes, DVDs, and vinyl records where Bruce could browse for hours. Then he would ask to go shopping at the mall because it was his birthday, and you can never have enough Champion, Nike, or Puma sweatpants and sweatshirts.

But this birthday would be more than presents. This

birthday would be a huge celebration Janice and I planned for Sunday, August 26. All of KenCrest was invited, no exaggerating; every group home received a birthday invitation. Anyone who knew Bruce in any capacity was invited, including people from dialysis, workshop, the library, and the bowling alley.

One wall of the basement housed a picture display that told Bruce's life story, arranged by Rafael, Bruce's longtime housemate, and me. Creating this collage was like walking back in time. I don't know who had more fun with this project: Rafael, Bruce, or me. I had forgotten how adorable David and Bruce were together. I chose his baby picture, the four-year-old Bruce on drums, and Bruce chose a picture with the two of us to be used for his birthday cake. He and I got tuna hoagies (his favorite from Wawa), and because superheroes was the theme, giant Spiderman balloons greeted the guests outside with Batman and Superman inside.

I left for the house early to help set up. Big Bruce and Jerica came later. Bruce's recliner from his bedroom was brought down the basement for our guest of honor smack in the center of the room. Cedric set up his equipment to DJ this event with the birthday cake and snacks nearby. Food cooked especially for the party was set upstairs. What a day. Our picture wall was a great success with all of the guests. So many people knew who I was —some I had not seen in years and did not remember. It was humbling to have these people appreciate David and my involvement with Bruce, asking how David was even though he had moved to Florida so long ago.

Bruce shared and spoke about us as much as we shared and spoke about him. Some siblings speak (or not), grow apart, move and never visit, but here was proof of our undeniable bond and commitment to a baby forged 50 years ago by a nine-year-old and thirteen-year-old, through college, marriages, divorces, children, summer vacations, work, and long-distance moves. Captain and Tennille sang it best: "Love will keep us together." Although David and Lisa could not be there in person, this gorgeous edible fruit plant arrived with balloons of—you guessed it—superheroes. It definitely added to the festivities and Bruce's excitement.

Having retired, my new schedule allowed for flexibility and inclusion with Bruce's doctor visits and Individual Plan meetings. Even in these environments, my identity was known.

"Oh, Bruce who do we have here? Is this Lynne?"

"Yes, it is," Bruce would answer with a grin, eyes bright while hugging me. Or "You must be the infamous big sister in New Jersey," or "We've heard so much about you and David who lives in Florida." My favorite was: "Bruce, you didn't tell us your sister was pretty." She's not pretty," he exclaimed with his face scrunched up and we all burst out laughing. "She's beautiful." That shut everyone up, including me.

Big Bruce and I retired in June and October of 2017 respectively so that we could focus on readying the house for the market by March 2018. As my un-move plan had faltered, in a last-ditch attempt, I reasoned that Florida summers were unbearable, especially for someone who hates the heat—my husband. We would be air-conditioning dependent, never enjoying the outside, which would make me miserable. "Agreed. Where would you like us to spend our summers?" He offered. Without hesitation I answered, "Vail, Colorado, in the Rockies where my heart sings." My husband owned a timeshare in Vail Village and we had spent a few summer vacations there hiking, horseback riding, and white water rafting, some of my favorite sports activities. Well aware of Vail's high real estate pricing, my plan of not moving to Florida looked brighter. I had agreed to spend two weeks of August prior to retiring that following June in Vail shopping for a summer home, confident that something in our price range would never be found. It turns out I was clearly underestimating Bruce's and the real estate agent's relentless determination to make me happy. Bruce and Doug had been corresponding for months with prospects ready for our perusal upon arrival to the timeshare. Doug and his wife Erin, a dynamo team and now dear friends, devised a succinct productive plan taking into consideration my desire of close proximity to the Village. I wanted the flexibility of walking or taking the bus, not dependency on a car.

They did it. They found an adorable two-story condo in East Vail, four miles from the Village, walkable through the golf course or mountain trail, or by bus down the street from us. Gore Creek was right outside of our second-floor entrance, and The Gore Mountains were a short walk from my downstairs front door. "Well honey, what do you have to say?" asks Bruce. Looking up at him, stunned, to say the least, after a long sigh I said, "I'll be damned. I guess I'm moving to Florida." I was willing to change my original plan of never moving to Florida, to a modified plan of winter in Florida and summer in Vail. What a life. Who in their right mind would complain?

We had to prepare to sell the house. Fortunately, I started working part-time, twenty-five hours per week tutoring math and language arts for Learn It Systems to get me out of the house when renovation work began. To say I am not one who handles the inconvenience of strangers ripping my home apart well is the understatement of the century. Our handyman Scott, who has become a dear friend over the years, resurfaced our kitchen cabinets, redid our downstairs powder room, and built pull-down stairs from our ceiling into the attic. Each small, contained job performed by a man of whom I am very fond will attest to my unhappiness during said endeavors. Big Bruce, while having the patience of a flea, thrived on checking progress, negotiating with contractors, reveling in correcting incompetence and visiting with Scott. A true match made in heaven. Although miserable, I must admit that the upgrades we had chosen (the new carpeting in the living room and on the stairs, and the hard wood flooring in the dining room and kitchen) were gorgeous, making me realize we should have done these long ago for our own enjoyment, not the new owners. Shame on us!

Little Bruce did not handle these changes well either, confused by what was happening in our home, the packed boxes in the garage labeled Florida and the ones in the living room labeled Vail. You see, we weren't going to be making only one move to Florida. (Oh, no! Why go simple?) Homes were not selling well in our Voorhees neighborhood, hence putting the house on the market in March. Our Plan A was for our agent Deb Sable to show the house and sell it in August while we spent the summer driving across the country to Vail, leisurely spending two weeks to explore the United States before officially moving into our new condo. We would return to Voorhees in September to make settlement and drive to Florida in November arriving December 1. If it did not sell by August, Plan B would be trying again the following March. These best laid plans were not to be.

Deb, also now a good friend, was and is amazing. Our home sold in three days with only one formal showing. The predicament: we could not go to Vail until June because we had renters until May 30, nor could we move to Florida as the lease there ended November 30. Thank goodness the new buyers were not quite ready to move until June.

Our updated Plan C meant moving three times. The

dining room was now labeled "The Vista," holding the things that would go to an apartment near the house, close to Brucie. It was a first-floor, one-bedroom, one-bathroom rental apartment that would act as a three-month holding cell for rental furniture from September to November. Everything in the dining room could be packed in my car and would be staying with our friends Steve and Dori until our return in September. (Packing and planning for three moves is oh-so-much fun.) The boxes in the garage labeled "Florida" would now be placed in a storage facility through our moving company from June until November to be loaded into the moving truck for a December 5 arrival. The living room remained the only constant, holding everything we would need to pack in Bruce's SUV for Vail. Exhausting right? This all took place a little over two years ago and writing about it is just as exhausting.

Not wanting to tell my brother about leaving and to keep him distracted, we went through all of the clothes closets and made three piles: Vail, what to keep, what to give away. He wrote the words on large sheets of paper and proceeded to go shopping in the closets while I contributed to the piles, making a fourth pile labeled Brucie. I did explain that we would be spending the summer in the mountains. I showed him Colorado on a map and pictures of Vail Village, Vail Mountain, and our condo, which were all surrounded by Gore Creek, Gore Mountain Range, wooded trails, and Aspen trees. I would not realize the impression these photos would make until much later while living at the Vista.

Brucie remained our source of entertainment through the stress of packing and all of the moving arrangements. Each Sunday, he helped with packing and taping boxes and distracted me with walks. "How about we go to the lake. You need a rest," he suggested a few times. Then, while unpacking boxes, I heard him say, "Ooohhh. I like this."

"Bruce! I just filled that. What are you doing?" I asked exasperated.

"What? What I do? I shopping." Rolling my eyes, I just laughed, unable to muster real frustration with the innocence of the situation. He happily continued "shopping" while Big Bruce and I finished our goal for the day.

June arrived, and I greeted the movers with mixed emotions. The first leg of the journey was our trip to Vail. This would be difficult for me as this would be the longest Brucie and I had ever been without seeing each other. It would be almost four months, and not just him, but Janice, Ms. Lee, and the guys—my extended family whom I love dearly. FaceTime is a great substitute, but just not the same. I took extensive photos of our two-week stretch, sending them to Janice faithfully, and keeping everyone involved with our trip and experiences. My brother was especially enthralled with the Rock and Roll Hall of Fame in Ohio, our baseball catches at the Field of Dreams in Iowa, and The Greyhound Hall of Fame in Abilene, Kansas. (Remember our greyhounds, Bazooka, Ion, and Brenda?)

Vail was wonderful. The mountains truly make my heart sing and it sang all summer. Standing at the top of Vail Mountain looking out over the Sawatch Mountain Range, I know that living here even only part time is one of the best decisions I have ever made.

When our time to return back east approached, it was with mixed emotions that we packed to leave. I missed my brother and my grandchildren, so with a heavy heart, we begin our journey home knowing our next adventure. The Vista would be challenging with only one bathroom, and even less space than our condo. My husband and I had only dealt with limited accommodations for one week of vacation. I figured that if we could handle packing for three moves, driving 2700 miles for two weeks across the country, and staying in a variety of hotel rooms along the way, how much harder could this be? We would soon find out and I just couldn't wait! (I do make myself laugh.)

We made the trip home to New Jersey in three and a half days, retrieved my car, and settled into the Vista with minimal complications as I had reviewed all ordered rental furniture with CORT Furniture Rental while on the road home. I also confirmed getting my brother that Sunday, excited to talk to everyone at his group home. Having a sharp eye for landscape and landmarks, Bruce said, "Lynne, where are we?" he abruptly interrupted our conversation after crossing the Betsy Ross Bridge and taking an unrecognized turn, "Where are we going?"

"To our apartment, honey. Remember, we don't live in our house anymore." How would he remember all those packed boxes from months ago? He wasn't with us when the movers removed all of the furniture and the boxes from the garage, leaving the house empty. Nodding his head with an "Oh yes, yes," he responded. Having no reason to doubt his answer, we continued our conversation peppered with questions of the new landscape he was witnessing once we got off the new I-95 exit. His excitement grew, mixed with confusion and repetitive questions about our old house. "Why did you leave? Where are we going?" Once we pulled into the parking lot, "Oh, this is soooooo big," he breathed and giggled. Our unit was in the first of the three buildings facing us, each with six units and three floors. "Yes, we are in this building right in front of you, on the first floor," I told him while getting him to read the building number as we walked arm in arm down the few steps to my front door. We then read the apartment number so he could learn how to find it himself walking from the car on all following visits.

Brucie could not wait to see Big Bruce. Their reunion was very sweet to watch. "So, show me around," my brother requested. We laughed as this 800 square-foot space was, well, small. He took my arm and I walked him through the kitchen as he oohed and aahed over the stove, built-in tiny washer/dryer combo unit, bedroom, and tiny patio overlooking our wooded courtyard. "Take a picture of me here!" he exclaimed walking out onto the patio. I complied, snapping his different poses. "I take one of you, now."

"Let's take one together, a selfie," I offered, not comfortable turning my iPhone over to his care. "Yes. Stand like this," he commanded while I snapped the first of many selfies. "Now, listen to me. Put your arm around my shoulder. Come on, take the picture." He continued to pose the two of us for the next fifteen minutes, holding my hand with the camera and snapping the shots, too impatient to wait for me to actually focus the camera, changing our positions upon his approval of the finished product. "You are taking too long," he would say, or "Yech, that is terrible. Do it again." And finally, "Okay, I like this one. Send it to Janice. Tell her I took these." I had created a selfie monster.

It took a while for the novelty of this first visit to wear off with Brucie still asking about our old house, new directions, and why we sold the house. Finally, we settled out on the patio listening to his favorite musical requests and singing along to Springsteen, the Rolling Stones, and Joni Mitchell. Eventually, we came back in and sat at the dining room table so he could write in his journal, I was trying to ease him back into our Sunday routine. I had those first selfies printed for Brucie's photo album that I started so he could have us with him after our final move to Florida.

The next Sunday I came for Bruce, and he greeted me with, "You are late." He tapped his wristwatch, stalking to the couch to sit and sulk. Mind you, my brother could not tell time but had always been a stickler for being on time. Another thing we have in common. If he was told you would be there at 3:00 p.m., he would ask what that looked like on a clock. If he needed to be ready by 3:00 (taking forever to get ready with constant reminders, prodding, nudging, and check-ins—keep in mind our walks together and his lack of focus), you had better be there when the small hand is on the three and the big hand is on the twelve. He stood at the window watching so you could not fool him with a story. I was five minutes late, something that had never happened before, so I tried to be serious and apologetic with no success. I sat down on his lap and pretended to cry on his shoulder to hide my laughing. True to form, not being able to deal with my being upset, Bruce hugged me, "Lynnie, I'm sorry, I'm sorry," while rubbing my back. "Bruce, I promise I will never be late again," I said.

Once in the car the conversation began: "I don't know where my Nike sweatpants are." Some things never change. "Bruce, they are probably in the laundry." His "loss" of clothes was a constant complaint each Sunday because he did not like throwing his favorite pants or tops into the laundry. He would try to hide them just so he could wear them every day.

"Bruce I am not talking about your laundry." The conversation continued to go downhill as I told him he would be helping me do our laundry, figure out what's for dinner, and about Jerica, Randy and the apartment. "Ugh, again," he moaned, rolling his eyes, his head in his hands. With a deep sigh he said, "Alright, if I have to." Laughing, I replied, "What do you mean if you have to? Where else are we going to go?

"Lynnie, listen to me."

"I am listening."

"We have to go to your house."

"Why do we have to go to the house?"

"Because you have to."

I realized that Bruce didn't understand we no longer lived in that house, and he still did not appreciate what this apartment represented to him. This Sunday visit would encompass laundry and some new challenges to keep his interest while establishing our old routines of rolling and counting coins, journal writing, and reading. I only had three months to maintain these habits established in his Independent Learning Plan before leaving him. Our one-stop washer/dryer was too small for towels and heavier winter clothes so Brucie would have to accompany me to the second-floor laundry room. This meant carrying laundry baskets, laundry detergent, fabric softener, and coins for the washing machine and dryer up two levels of stairs and then learning new directions for their use. Keeping in mind his familiarity with the different coins, I asked, "Brucie, we need three quarters, two dimes, and one nickel."

"How about I put in the clothes and you do the money" was his reply. My answer with an edge of sarcasm was, "How about you put in the money, clothes, and detergent while I go downstairs and listen to music?" He grinned with a shrug, "Fine." Once everything was complete before walking down the stairs back to the apartment, I saw him gazing out of the large second floor hallway window. "How about you take a picture of me here," he said. Not sure I understood, "In the hallway?" I asked. "Yes, at the window. Like this. I'm ready." He struck a pose and, of course, I complied, shaking my head.

"Now, listen to me," Bruce moved me in front of the window, "You stand like this and I take our picture." He posed us together with confidence and snapped more selfies for Janice. "Send these to Janice. Go ahead, I'm waiting," he said waving his hand to move me along with this assigned task. "Let's send these to Mom and Dad also," I suggested. "Oh, good. How about we all have dinner here?" he asked.

"Honey, where do Mom and Dad live?"

"In Florida," he replied.

I asked, "So we can fly to Florida to see them and have dinner, right?" His face crumbled, "I not flying to Florida!" as he shook his head, waving his hand. Then he said, "Lynnie, I know. How about they come to Colorado?"

"Okay, everyone can have dinner with us in Colorado. You know, you have to fly to Colorado also?" I told him, surprised and confused by his request. "Sure," he said while linking his arm in mine to walk back. Steering me past the apartment he said, "Let's walk out here." He pulled me towards the courtyard. Arms still linked, we strolled the grounds, stopping at each piece of installed exercise equipment along the path for him to check out its use, finally returning, taking at least ten more selfies along the way.

Once inside, Brucie walked to the middle of the living room, stood in front of Big Bruce and exclaimed, "I just love your new place!" My husband, shocked by this proclamation as he detested living here, asked sarcastically, "Really, what exactly could you possibly like?" The totally unexpected response he gave us was, "Colorado is so beautiful." We laughed then as we still do today, remembering Brucie and realizing that his questions and obsession with pictures finally made sense. Just so you can understand some of his learning limitations, the Vista was less than two miles down the road from the home he had spent twenty-nine years visiting, which was also in the woods.

At the Vista, we either walked the trails or sat out in that courtyard in the cold, rain, or shine. Brucie sent Janice his pictures while he was with me. As far as he was concerned, these new woods, trails, and much smaller living space (which is actually what made me go *away* to Colorado for three months after our stay there), looked like the photos of Colorado that I had sent to Janice. This is why he was willing to fly to Colorado and not Florida. I was "there" and not in Florida. Therefore, he "had to be visiting Colorado soon." My brother was so enthralled with this alternate universe that he had us walking the courtyard of the Vista with snow falling in the bitter cold —parkas and scarves covering our faces and ski hats on our heads—just to send Janice pictures of "Vail, Colorado, in winter." Brucie hated the cold, but apparently, "winter in Colorado was okay." I met more neighbors in those three months there than I had met in the twenty-nine years living in my development because of my brother and his love of our "Colorado home."

Getting back to our laundry, it was time to tackle the dryer. More coins and moving the clothes across the room. My brother rose to the occasion and insisted on moving the clothes himself by demanding, "I got this." First, he tried grabbing a huge armful and moving it, dropping a few items on the floor. He looked at me and I just stood quietly—no easy feat. "Oops," he whispered, bringing the clothes back. I have to give him credit; he figured out putting the clothes in our empty basket, walking the basket to the machine, and then filling the machine. I was so proud as was he, giggling and giving me a big hug. Laundry became one of his favorite chores.

November was approaching and so was my last opportunity to participate, in person, in Bruce's Individual Learning Plan meeting. I so enjoyed these meetings, held at the workshop, where I could have an extra visit with Bruce, as he participated in these meetings also. Bruce would take me on tours, proudly showing off his "workplace," and introducing me to his co-workers. We engaged with educational professionals to create measurable goals for learning life skills that applied to his workshop and living in his group home. We also visited with some of my favorite people, those who were the most influential in his life and his care.

These meetings also gave me a chance to visit with Janice and other members of Bruce's group home who I did not usually get to see on my Sunday visits. This meeting would prove the most challenging as the day began with early morning snow, which became a full-blown storm during our meeting. Schools were closing early and so were the workshops for KenCrest residents, meaning that everyone at this meeting was needed elsewhere. Bruce was able to eat some of his lunch before we headed out into the storm. I had volunteered to take him home, underestimating the snow and traffic. The trip took two hours of skidding, sliding, and frozen windshield wipers. Thank goodness there was good music on the radio along with Bruce giving driving instructions from the show Dukes of Hazzard: "Lynnie, jump the car."

"Brucie, I can barely see, and my car does not do that."

"Oh, come on," he insisted waving his hands up in the air. "Just press this and jump," he exclaimed, reaching over to press buttons on the steering wheel. He continued to keep me entertained, singing to music and using my phone to call Janice. At that point I had just gotten Bluetooth, so imagine Brucie's reaction to my car talking to him once Janice answered her phone. "Hi, Lynne," Janice answered. "Janice, this is Bruce. The Acura is talking, it's talking. The car is talking." He laughed manically, "I called you and the car is talking." I let out my deep sigh and said, "Its magic!" Janice and I laughed as we checked in with each other as she was driving in this mess also. "Lynne, the car talks to you, too," giggled my brother. We ended our call and Bruce decided he needed more. "How about we call Big Bruce?" To totally blow his mind, I asked my car to call Big Bruce, his number being programmed into the system. Little Bruce just stared at me. When my husband answered, before I could say anything, "Big Bruce," my brother shouted, "The car called you." After assuring my husband we were safe even with the treacherous roads, he continued his conversation with Brucie. Little Bruce went on about how I refused to jump the car. The two of us finally reached Linden Avenue, said goodbye, and I resumed my travels home, another three-and-a-half-hour drive. Each Sunday visit after that drive, any time spent in the car included having my Acura call people so they could experience the magic of my talking car. To be that innocent and easy to please.

And so, the time came for our official move. One of the hardest things I have ever done was leaving Brucie. I was the only blood relative left up north. And how I was going to miss my Linden Avenue family. Even though we had spent the summer apart, this was different; this was final. Janice had been part of my life since 1988. Thirty years. She shared care for Bruce at doctor appointments, and she was there while he was in the hospital with pneumonia, at Jerica's birth, and at weddings. Ms. Lee and I spent many happy hours on Sunday mornings discussing politics, family, world news, and life. That last Sunday visit was gut wrenching, Brucie was the only one not crying.

The move was successful. I must admit that wearing shorts in December, January, and February; lying out by the neighborhood pool directly across the street from our home; and having celebrated my sixty-fifth birthday in December with a pool party were all pretty spectacular things to experience. I was able to visit with my mother on a regular basis, sometimes coordinating with David, Lisa, Randy, Laurie, and the girls for extra family time. We did see our grandchildren often with long weekend sleepover visits. Maddie and Emily were in charge of dinner, seasoning, and rolling homemade meatballs—and eating pancakes with sprinkles out on the patio early Sunday morning.

Having been separated for so long, Bruce and I were pleased to host the Passover Seder our first April in Florida, having all nine of us once more around my dining room table. Then we stayed in Vail that summer, planning on returning to host everyone in September for Rosh Hashanah, not knowing that Passover would be the last family visit to include my mother. My mom passed away July of 2019 while Randy and his family were visiting us in Vail. Brucie took the news well, knowing his mom and dad would be together in heaven.

"MY BABY IS GRADUATING MEDICAL SCHOOL," I sang while getting ready at our Airbnb. This time, our visit back to Philadelphia would be longer to celebrate Jerica's graduation from Temple University Medical School and her birthday. We had just been back to Philadelphia in March for Jerica's Match Day. Houston Methodist in Houston, Texas, would be her new home for the next five years as a surgical resident.

We got to visit Bruce and Janice, whom we hadn't seen since December. My first hug was heaven. Jerica was able to score four tickets so Bruce and Janice could join us for the graduation held at the Kimmel Center. Bruce—ever the photo hound—was so impressed with this venue that he had us posing together, separately, with Jerica, and with her friends he had just met. He introduced himself, "I'm Bruce and I'm going to college later." It was so sweet to watch his excitement for Jerica. After all, she was the only niece he had seen on a regular basis for the past ten years. He spent quality time with Randy's family each Christmas visit and with David and Lisa during their yearly family holiday visit, but Jerica was a constant, coming to all holiday dinners and as many Sunday dinners as her schedule allowed.

He was quiet during the ceremony and the Dalai Lama's speech but yelled with us when Jerica's name was called. The fun continued through the celebratory luncheon and into the next day with the four of us bowling. I knew Bruce loved to bowl since he was a young child, but I had no idea my brother bowled in a bowling league. He had his own ball with a matching bag, gloves, and shoes, of course. He was pretty good, better than Jerica and me, and told Big Bruce how to keep score. He cheered when he recognized his name and Jerica's up on the big screen. Big Bruce destroyed all of us. We shared pizza, soda, and snacks just like the old days before we moved. It was a great weekend and hard to leave not knowing when we would see Bruce and Janice next.

Bruce's favorite holidays are Thanksgiving (mine too), Rosh Hashanah, and Passover. I appreciate Thanksgiving, football games, and the smell of turkey and stuffing permeating the house with family soon to follow. My mother, loving family but never one to enjoy the art of cooking, was thrilled to abdicate the responsibility to me for all family holidays. That's right, all. Having no sister or aunts and with both parents being only children, my home was the welcoming haven, no matter the size at any particular time. Cooking for my family was not very successful in my younger married years. (Too many burnt meals to expound upon. Perhaps my next book.) It had, however, turned into one of my greatest joys and, I might boast, one of my special talents. So, what a blessing having control of the menu, environment, and participants.

Bruce was guaranteed inclusion, not just with his family for the meal, but also the preparation of the meal and the entire essence of the day. He loved to cook, standing over my shoulder to season and, of course, taste. I would get him early in the day, looking forward to spending our 45-minute ride catching up, just the two of us. It was Randy, Jerica, and their uncle, who was almost like a big brother—all three helping with cooking, setting the table, making place cards, and sharing pre-dinner snacks before anyone else arrived.

My children were raised to appreciate the importance of inclusion, especially during the holidays. Holidays are hard for many people, particularly those with no family and few friends. Our family motto is, "No one spends any holiday alone." Taking this to heart, Randy and Jerica invited anyone suspected of having nowhere to go. Many times, I would have unexpected guests for any given holiday and learned to cook for the legions, earning the nickname America's Hostess from my husband. My brother, always the charmer hearing the doorbell would exclaim, "OH!! Who do we have now?" His audience of admirers growing with his swelled head.

When Bruce was very young, our neighbors were afraid of him. The same people who were my parents' friends who helped raise us, their children being our friends, ran away or closed their doors when I brought Bruce outside to join games. This tiny defenseless two-year-old terrified them and made them uncomfortable. My heart was shattered. The drive to rectify this had begun. My plan to include Bruce was to open his world. We accomplished so much more, my baby brother and I. We opened theirs.

Our extended family asked for Bruce regularly, wanting to understand Down's Syndrome and kidney disease. My children's friends were disappointed if it was an off weekend when they hung out together, having brought tapes of Bruce's favorite music. He was our family, so naturally, he was part of theirs. Amazing what minds that are opened can accomplish.

We had lived in Florida for about two years now and no matter how we tried, we were unsuccessful in getting Brucie to come visit. He was willing to visit Colorado, but never Florida. Due to his health issues, Vail, Colorado, with its hills, mountains, and high altitude of 8,150 feet—and East Vail where we live being 8,500 feet—was not conducive for him. We talked often and FaceTimed, but I would have loved to have had him here to see my mother before she died and visit with David, Lisa, and my children. I missed having him for Thanksgiving and our shopping excursions for his birthday and Hanukkah. I did honor his gift requests, delighting in his excited phone calls when he received his presents.

CHAPTER 7

Back to the End

"Lynne, where are you?" I was brought back to the moment with Brucie asking me for ginger ale. "What's wrong? Are you okay?"

"Nothing is wrong, love. Just thinking about when you were little," I answered. This satisfied him. "Listen to me! I would like some ginger ale, please." I went to the kitchen for the ginger ale smiling at his intuitiveness that most people seem to lack. I knew Brucie was terminal and would probably die within the next six months, but at this moment in time, I was grateful for his love and the gift of him. I got to be his guardian as it was always meant to be.

We returned to Vail. Bruce was getting out of bed more often and socializing with his housemates. He called me between three and four times a week. We FaceTimed when we could. Sometimes he would call at 5:00 a.m. or 5:30 a.m. Mountain Time and say, "Lynne, it's your brother, Bruce." He would state very seriously, "I would like to listen to James Taylor's (blah, blah, blah...)." Of course, I couldn't always understand him the first go-around, having just raced up the stairs half asleep, jolted out of bed by the ringing phone. "Brucie, slow down and tell me again." The infamous deep sigh and clearing of the throat followed by,

"Listen to me."

That expression will forevermore make me smile, "I would like to listen to James Taylor's 'Sweet Baby James.'" By this time, I would understand his request of me. Inevitably, I would ask to speak with whomever was on duty, pleased when Ms. Lee would come to the phone.

"You do realize it is only five in the morning here, right?" I reminded her.

"Yes," she acknowledged, "But I can't say no to him and I love talking to you."

How could I possibly remain annoyed, talking to two people I loved before the sun had yet to rise? It was always a nice way to start the day, especially as Brucie sounded so "healthy."

His dialysis schedule changed once more, adding back in the third day due to high fluid retention. The number of hours for each session were limited to three instead of four due to low blood pressure and low blood count. Unfortunately, Bruce would need another transfusion, but understanding the fact that he would only stay in the hospital one night and that someone would be with him, he was amiable.

By October, the cancer was really taking its toll. He was having trouble keeping food down and he was having bathroom accidents. Another visit was planned in spite of COVID and my husband, who was dealing with AFib with

serious heart palpitations and was scheduled for an abla-
tion, a heart procedure to fix his wiring. This visit, we
stayed at an Airbnb within walking distance of the hospital. Of course, my brother, true to form, overhearing my
conversation with Jerica about her father, beckoned Big
Bruce over to his bed. "What does that mean, your heart?
How are you feeling? Are you good? How about you lay
here and take a nap?" No matter how lousy he felt, he
wasn't happy that someone he cared for could be sick. He
remembered our mother had died from having a sick
heart. I shake my head and marvel, not the first time, at his
capacity to love, his capacity to just go on because there
was no other choice.

Along with "Listen to me," "What does that mean?" is
another expression we all use, another Bruceism to keep us
smiling. Randy texted me before our FaceTime call: "Emily
and I are watching a movie and she just told me the main
character reminds her of Uncle Bruce." (Yes, we will all
keep him in our memories and hearts.)

We had stayed in Vail through the end of October,
longer than usual, in case Brucie needed us again. My
brother remained stable for the time being. We began
packing for our return trip back to Florida. Never having
been in the Rockies for fall, this extended visit was a gift
and afforded me the opportunity to witness my Aspens
changing color and traipse through nine inches of snow
along my favorite trail up the mountain to say goodbye.

By the time we arrived in Florida on November 3, my
brother had rallied slightly, still in bed, but he was talking
on the phone with enthusiasm, calling me regularly and
wanting to Facetime. But his numbers continued to cause
concern, and Justina, his palliative nurse, called early
Friday morning, November 13, to let me know he would
be going to the hospital upon the recommendation of his
primary care physician, Janice, who was by his side the

whole time. Immediately following that call, my husband and I had looked into flights to Philadelphia. We would fly in Saturday morning nonstop as Friday night flights had a layover. Flying for the third time was dangerous enough. We were at the store in the early afternoon purchasing K95 masks for the trip when I took that dreaded call from a Jefferson Hospice nurse. "Lynne, I am so sorry, but we don't know if your brother will make it through the night."

My heart hurt for Janice, who had to hear that news alone. After making some calls, my KenCrest family rallied, coming to stay with Janice and Brucie until we got there. Paperwork was completed on my end to place him in acute hospice care, meaning morphine every four hours for pain, waiting for him to pass.

Ever the trooper, Brucie rallied late Friday night, calling David and me, excited to be feeling better. "Hi, Lynne. I feel good. I want to go home." I was relieved to hear his voice, confident he would be alive on Saturday, praying he might be able to come home for in-home hospice. This was not to be.

Big Bruce and I arrived at the hospital Saturday, happy to hug and cry with Janice and kiss my brother, squeezing his hand. "I love you," I whispered. Although he was sleeping, he squeezed back letting me know he knew I was there. Janice was now able to leave. Big Bruce and I spent the evening chatting with Brucie, playing his favorite music, and talking with David and Lisa. Unfortunately, he never fully regained consciousness. I stayed through the night, letting him know he was loved, holding his hand and rubbing his arm to soothe him when he got agitated. Big Bruce returned Sunday morning—my knight in shining armor—with coffee, fruit, and cheese as the hospital cafeteria was closed due to COVID.

Brucie passed away Sunday night on November 15, peacefully in his sleep. I feel blessed to have been with him, watching him take his final breath, his hand warm in mine. I whispered to my husband, "Honey, Brucie has..." My husband whispered with me, "...stopped breathing." He was watching as well.

I kissed Brucie goodbye, feeling an immense emptiness mixed with relief at his quick passing, knowing this would be the last time I would see him—ever. This small, sweet man who had such a profound influence on my life as no other. He had survived exactly four months from the date of his diagnosis, just as the oncologist had thought. Who knows how long he actually had cancer before getting diagnosed?

I spoke with the funeral director that evening so arrangements could be made to get my brother to the morgue. Early Monday morning, final burial arrangements were made, and we left for Linden Avenue to begin the arduous process of cleaning his room and choosing burial clothes. We also had to pack what would be donated to the Veterans Association, to Rafael and Bill, to KenCrest, and what would be shipped to Florida for family. My husband, Ms. Lee, Janice, and I were a formidable team. Through tears and laughter, we were able to choose his burial clothes, not an easy feat as everything my brother wore had to match. Imagine three grown, accomplished women, his big sisters, fretting over what Brucie would want to wear. Most sisters argue about money or who their parents loved more. Not us. We did agree on Champion sweats, no formal suit.

"OH, that won't do. No, no, no—he won't like that. The bottoms are too tight," argued Ms. Lee.

"The funeral director told me shoes are not necessary," I explained to her, "The Man Who Would Be Sneaker King would roll in his grave. Take these sneakers. The white and black match his top and bottom." I offered my two cents.

"Listen," Janice piped in, "We need black sneaker socks, not white if he's gonna wear those sneakers."

I learned that he gave Stephen a hard time and refused to be taken to the hospital that Friday morning until he found the perfect sweatshirt to match his sweatpants. We then focused on his room. Taking a much-needed break, Bruce, Janice, and I delivered his clothes to the funeral home, stopped at the cemetery to finalize the site and ordered food for *shiva*, the Jewish mourning period for immediate family, to be held at Linden Avenue following the funeral. After all, where better and who better to mourn and celebrate Brucie's life with than our extended family in their home?

We returned to finish our packing and left that evening for the UPS store to ship our boxes of memories back to Florida. The door to Brucie's room remained closed. It was too difficult to see this finality of emptiness.

Not having a local rabbi, one was shared by the funeral parlor, with whom I spoke Sunday evening. We began our conversation as strangers, only to learn he knew my parents and David. "Lynne, I need to ask. Ezersky is not a common name. Do you know a man named Izzy?" I chuckled. "Yes, he was my father." Even from the grave, everyone knew my father. I knew the rabbi's parents, but we were a few too many years apart to know each other. *Bashert* is Yiddish for destiny. Not every rabbi would serve a family not affiliated with their temple. How lucky were we to have him?

His next question was not so easy to answer: "Lynne, what four words would you use to describe your brother Bruce?" *Really?* I thought, rolling my eyes, thankful he could not see me. Just four words? *Cute, funny, loving, fashionista* all came to mind, but would not suffice. "Rabbi," I sigh, "Four words just won't work. I realize this could possibly help much, so let me share some memories instead." If crying is truly good for the soul, the next hour spent reminiscing with the rabbi cleansed me for the next decade. I ended our trip down memory lane, which had been peppered with amazingly intuitive questions from the rabbi, with these last words: "To know Bruce was to love him."

"MY FINAL QUESTION," promised the rabbi, "Will you have family with you?"

I needed this kind man to appreciate the family he would be meeting at the funeral service. "I will be surrounded by family," I boasted, "Not related by blood, but love and choice and not related by religion, but by faith in each other."

My eulogy at the funeral service was comprised of thank yous for my extended family—thirty of them—who braved COVID and the cold to stand with me; for my husband, who spoke lovingly of his brother-in-law; for David, Lisa, and our rabbi for truly listening to my stories about Brucie and the family standing with me that Bruce had created, as reflected by the service and stories we told that day. Our plans for Brucie were to open and enrich his world. Oh, but being with Bruce accomplished so much more. He opened the world to us, enriching our lives. What more could be asked of one soul with a great big heart? I also included a quote from Mr. Rogers, summing up Bruce's outlook on life and effect on people: "Mutual caring relationships require kindness and patience, tolerance, optimism, joy in the other's achievements, confidence in oneself, and the ability to give without undue thought of gain." Brucie, we are still listening!

Bruce, the rabbi, and I waited for everyone to participate in the final ritual of shoveling dirt onto the grave before leaving the cemetery. We would be returning to

Linden Avenue for *shiva* and the celebration of Bruce's life. "Lynne," the rabbi interrupted my thoughts, "I know you told me you would be surrounded by family. I am overwhelmed. I have been doing this for years and have never felt such warmth, such love, as today." My smile was my only answer.

Shiva was exactly as I requested: a life celebration. La-toya, ever ready to respect and support my needs, supplied our group with five bottles of pink champagne. We shared many memories, laughed and cried, but never lost sight of the positive light my brother had shone on all of us.

REFLECTIONS

MY FINAL CHAT WITH GOD

"So, my dear. That is not a happy face," God says. My eyes narrow and I point my finger at his chest. "It appears as though we still have unfinished business."

"Yes," I breathe.

"Ah. Still not satisfied with my initial answer as to the *why* of Bruce."

I just glare.

"I've always been charmed by that look of yours," God chuckles. "You have become who you are because of Bruce." Continuing in a more serious and gentle tone, he says, "Yes, you love animals and would have been a great veterinarian. Yes, you almost flunked out of college, but you mastered psychology for your true purpose, and yes, you had to change your major, choosing fashion and design. You should thank me because you needed a reality check on your fashion sense."

I interrupt, "What do you mean, my true purpose?" and under my breath, "There is nothing wrong with my fashion sense."

God snorts but goes on, "Your path led you to teaching. Although this was the last profession on earth you wanted, look at what you have accomplished. You have taught and mentored hundreds of students and teachers. As a building administrator, how many lives have you touched and positively influenced? You may not have wanted education, but education wanted and needed you. This was your true purpose." It is hard to admit, but God is right. With tears running down my cheeks, I nod.

Almost in a whisper, he adds, "Thirty-one years working with children in the classroom, tutoring little ones after you retired and moved to Florida. Still being the voice for those who need help. Why did I give you Bruce? To save you, my dear. To save you."

ABOUT THE AUTHOR

Lynne Podrat graduated from the Pennsylvania State University and then spent fifteen years in the Fashion Industry as an Assistant Buyer and Department Manager with Bloomingdale's Department Store before returning to school to receive her educational degrees from Arcadia University and Gynedd Mercy. A retired educator and Administrator from the Philadelphia, Pennsylvania School District, she taught English, literature, composition and history in elementary and secondary schools. She has secretly been a writer and poet her whole life, but has only recently chosen to share those talents with the world. Lynne now lives with her husband in Palm Beach Gardens, Florida, spending summers hiking the Rockies in Vail, Colorado where her heart sings.

Listen To Me is Lynne's first book.

instagram.com/lynnepodratwrites

facebook.com/lynne.podrat

CPSIA information can be obtained
at www.ICGtesting.com
Printed in the USA
BVHW041847230821
615060BV00015B/772